"*Welcome to Manhood* is essential for any young man seeking to step into his full, God-given potential in a world that often settles for mediocrity. Noah Herrin speaks with a rare level of authentic wisdom that comes only from someone who walks the walk and has earned the trust of this generation. If you want to become the man your calling, family, and world desperately need—the kind who chooses integrity and embraces difficult challenges—then this book isn't just recommended; it's required reading."

Rich Wilkerson Jr., lead pastor of Vous Church, author and speaker

"In a culture that confuses strength with dominance and manhood with passivity, the assault on men has never been louder. The enemy knows that if he can take down the men, he can take down the family. *Welcome to Manhood* is a bold call to rise above the lies. My friend Noah doesn't coddle—he challenges. He calls men back to courage, character, and conviction. So, men of today, if you're tired of sitting on the sidelines and ready to lead with strength, fight for what matters, and love like a man should love—this is your start here."

Madison Prewett Troutt, bestselling author, speaker and podcast host

welcome to manhood

Books by Noah Herrin

From Bethany House Publishers and Chosen Books

Welcome to Manhood:
Moving from Potential to Purpose

Holy Habits:
10 Small Decisions That Lead to a Big Life

welcome to manhood

Moving from Potential to Purpose

_Noah Herrin

a division of Baker Publishing Group
Minneapolis, Minnesota

© 2025 by Herrin Ministries, Inc.

Published by Bethany House Publishers
Minneapolis, Minnesota
BethanyHouse.com

Bethany House Publishers is a division of
Baker Publishing Group, Grand Rapids, Michigan

Printed in the United States of America

All rights reserved. No part of this publication may be reproduced, stored in a retrieval system, or transmitted in any form or by any means—for example, electronic, photocopy, recording—without the prior written permission of the publisher. The only exception is brief quotations in printed reviews.

Library of Congress Cataloging-in-Publication Data
Names: Herrin, Noah, author.
Title: Welcome to manhood : moving from potential to purpose / Noah Herrin.
Description: Minneapolis, Minnesota : Bethany House Publishers, a division of Baker Publishing Group, [2025] | Includes bibliographical references.
Identifiers: LCCN 2024052461 | ISBN 9780764244766 (paperback) | ISBN 9780764245077 (casebound) | ISBN 9781493450848 (ebook)
Subjects: LCSH: Christian men—Religious life
Classification: LCC BV4528.2 .H467 2025 | DDC 248.8/42—dc23/eng/20250310
LC record available at https://lccn.loc.gov/2024052461

Unless otherwise indicated, Scripture quotations are from the Holy Bible, New International Version®, NIV®. Copyright © 1973, 1978, 1984, 2011 by Biblica, Inc.® Used by permission of Zondervan. All rights reserved worldwide. www.zondervan.com. The "NIV" and "New International Version" are trademarks registered in the United States Patent and Trademark Office by Biblica, Inc.®

Scripture quotations labeled CSB are from the Christian Standard Bible®, copyright © 2017 by Holman Bible Publishers. Used by permission. Christian Standard Bible® and CSB® are federally registered trademarks of Holman Bible Publishers.

Scripture quotations labeled ESV are from The Holy Bible, English Standard Version® (ESV®), copyright © 2001 by Crossway, a publishing ministry of Good News Publishers. Used by permission. All rights reserved. ESV Text Edition: 2016.

Scripture quotations labeled MSG are taken from THE MESSAGE, copyright © 1993, 2002, 2018 by Eugene H. Peterson. Used by permission of NavPress. All rights reserved. Represented by Tyndale House Publishers, Inc.

Scripture quotations labeled NKJV are from the New King James Version®. Copyright © 1982 by Thomas Nelson. Used by permission. All rights reserved.

Cover design by David Carlson, Studio Gearbox

The Proprietor is represented by A Drop of Ink LLC, www.adropofink.pub

Baker Publishing Group publications use paper produced from sustainable forestry practices and postconsumer waste whenever possible.

25 26 27 28 29 30 31   7 6 5 4 3 2 1

To Mila Madisyn Herrin

You changed my life.
A world with little ladies as precious as you deserves men
pursuing a higher standard.

foreword

In a time when the very essence of manhood is often questioned and misconstrued, Noah Herrin steps into the fray with a bold and timely message. As a pastor deeply rooted in Nashville, Tennessee, Noah has consistently demonstrated his gift for reaching and inspiring young audiences. His evangelistic fervor and commitment to the gospel shine through every word and action, making him a beacon of light in a world that so desperately needs it.

Our culture today is rife with confusion and conflict about what it means to be a man. The term *toxic masculinity* is frequently hurled about, often painted with broad strokes that miss the true calling of manhood as outlined in the Bible. In such an environment, young men are left wondering how to navigate their identities in a way that honors God while also contributing positively to society. This is where *Welcome to Manhood* becomes a crucial guide.

Noah's book does not shy away from the hard questions and the societal pressures that men face today. Instead, it confronts them head-on with the truth of God's Word and the example of Jesus Christ. Noah inspires us to reclaim a biblical vision of manhood that is neither domineering nor passive, but one that is rooted in strength, humility, and sacrificial love.

foreword

In these pages, you will find a clarion call to become God-fearing men, whether as husbands, fathers, or single contributors to society. Noah's passionate and practical insights will challenge and equip you to rise above the noise and to stand firm in your faith. He calls us to be men who are not afraid to lead with love, who are courageous enough to serve, and who are committed to living out the principles of the kingdom of God in every area of our lives.

As someone who has had the privilege of witnessing Noah's ministry up close, I can attest to his genuine heart for people and his unwavering dedication to the gospel. His message is not just for the young men he reaches so well, but for anyone seeking to understand and live out authentic manhood in today's world.

Welcome to Manhood is more than a book; it's a movement. It's an invitation to step into the fullness of what God has called us to be. I encourage you to read this book with an open heart and a willingness to be transformed. Let Noah Herrin's words spur you on to be the man God designed you to be—a man of faith, courage, and uncompromising integrity.

—Jonathan Pokluda

1_

a warning

This book is not for everyone.

No, seriously.

If you're looking for the easier, more comfortable, and more traveled path, you should probably close the book now and carry on with your day. I'm just warning you on the first page that this isn't a book that will tell you what you want to hear. This is a book that will tell you what you *need* to hear.

With every passing year, it seems as though the standard for men gets lowered. On television men are often portrayed as lazy, dumb pushovers who offer very little value to the world. It's clear that the world expects little from us. But what's truly heartbreaking is that, for many of us, we expect less of ourselves.

It's become normal to make excuses instead of taking ownership. It's become popular to cut corners instead of living lives of integrity. It's become celebrated to follow anyone and anything besides Jesus.

This book is not for those who are okay with the standard being lowered. It's not for those who crave popularity. It's not a self-help book. It's not a long motivational speech. It's not a book with perfectly formed paragraphs aimed toward enabling you to keep doing things that could well be killing your soul.

If you want any of these things, just put the book back on the shelf or regift it to someone else. But if you want to live a life that really counts, both in this life and the next one . . .

If you're frustrated by the standard of manhood that is currently acceptable to so many . . .

If you're not afraid of facing hard things . . .

If you want what is best for the people you love . . .

If you desire to leave this world a better place than how you found it . . .

If so, then welcome to manhood.

An explanation: For the last nine years, I've dedicated my life to teaching others about a man who changed my life, a man named Jesus. That man was the greatest man to ever walk this earth.

As I've walked with Him, I've learned a lot about manhood. I'm *still* learning a lot about manhood.

I'm about to turn thirty as I write this book. I have a long way to go on my journey to being the best man I can be. I didn't write this book as the "master Jedi" or "guru" on manhood. Far from it. I wrote this book because I wanted to help other men avoid some of the mistakes I've made as a young man. It's been said that experience is the greatest teacher. Who said it has to be your own experience, though?

I wrote this book seeking to help you on your own journey into manhood. I'm going to cover things like overcoming pornography, stepping into your calling, learning to disagree with others, and dozens of other topics—all from the perspective of growing as a man who's seeking to be like the greatest man of all time: Jesus.

In each chapter I'll present:

1. A problem. Something that men have to come face-to-face with.
2. A solution. Something that helps us to overcome, or fight, or equips us to deal with the problem.
3. A next step today. Something practical we can do right now in taking a step toward improvement.
4. A habit to work toward. Something that builds on the next step that can become a part of our routine.
5. A truth to believe. Something that's true, which we can trust and believe in as we journey toward being the men God has called us to be.

There are fifty-two chapters in this book. I did this intentionally so that you could read one chapter a week for the entire year. Take your time with this book. The material we're going to cover deserves time to soak into our spirits. Read it. Apply it. Talk about it with others. More importantly, talk about it with Jesus.

My prayer for you as you journey through this book is that one year from now, you will look back and be able to confidently say: I've become more like the man Jesus wants me to be.

Welcome to manhood.

—Noah Herrin

2

be a finisher

The Problem

Starting things is easy. Finishing things is hard.

Every January for years I had the same goal: get ripped. I dreamed of looking like a young Arnold Schwarzenegger with six-pack abs and bazooka biceps. I would always start strong! I'd lift weights, wake up early, and eat grass.

But then a few weeks in, my New Year's resolution always went into early retirement. According to *Time* magazine, over 80 percent of New Year's resolutions fail by February 1st! This represents our problem.

We aren't called to start; we're called to finish.

The Solution

The apostle Paul, the author of much of the New Testament, was obsessed with the idea of life being like a race. Several times in his writings he refers to us as runners and makes it clear that a runner's priority should be to FINISH the race.

In fact, at the end of his life, Paul victoriously wrote these famous words: "I have fought the good fight, I have finished the race, I have kept the faith" (2 Timothy 4:7).

Billy Graham, one of the greatest preachers of the gospel the world has ever seen, once said, "Our world is obsessed with success. But how does God define success? Success in God's eyes is faithfulness to His calling."

Paul and Billy Graham both believed the same thing. In the kingdom of God, faithfulness is success. Finishing is the goal. When we get to heaven one day, we will not hear, "Well done, my good and rich, famous and successful servant." Hopefully we will all hear, "Well done, my good and faithful servant."

You see, the world claps for starters, but heaven claps for finishers! When people finish what they started, they become living testimonies to the goodness and faithfulness of God. Thank God that Jesus didn't just start His mission, but He finished it! He is our supreme example.

When we finish what we started, other people will look at us and be inspired and intrigued at the same time because finishing is becoming more and more rare in our world. More importantly, they'll look at us and see something more inside of us: a living God who helped us keep running the race. Our lives as finishers will reflect the true finisher: Jesus Christ!

Our world needs more men who will finish what they started.

Finish what you say yes to.
Finish what God asks you to do.
Finish what God has called you to.
Finish raising your kids the best you can.
Finish your marriage faithfully.
Finish the race.

You were called to start. Yes!
But by the grace of God, you will be a finisher!

Next Step Today

Run with a group.

I'm one of those people who actually enjoys running. It's become one of my favorite hobbies. Even though I love to run, there are times when my body is screaming at me to cut a run short. My mind whispers, *You've already run two miles. Is the last mile really going to make that big of a difference?*

An interesting thing I've noticed is that my brain tells me to quit way more often when I'm running by myself. I don't know if it's my competitive nature, not wanting to let people down, or just enjoying the run more, but when I run with other people, I'm more likely to finish my workout! Running with others brings out the best in me, both mentally and physically.

It works the same way spiritually. If you want to increase your chances of finishing exponentially, run with a group.

Practically speaking, you need to find a few other men who have the same goal you have: to be a finisher. Start a group text, meet as often as possible, hold each other accountable, and root each other on.

I wonder how many men would have been finishers had they simply refused to run alone.

Habit to Work Toward

Check in once a week with your group of finishers, even if it's just for a few minutes.

Something like, "Hey, guys, how are you doing this week? How's the race going? Are there any obstacles in the way? How can I pray for you? Here's where I've done well, and here's where I haven't. Can you pray for me?"

Truth to Believe

Because Jesus finished His mission, I can finish mine. I'm not just a starter; I'm a finisher.

3_

chase the right goals

The Problem

I sat next to a man on an airplane who flew two million miles with the same airline.

The pilot's voice came on over the intercom and honored the man for his accomplishment. Everyone on the plane clapped for the man. But the man sitting next to me was not smiling.

He turned to me and said, "They're clapping for the very thing I regret the most."

I learned that because of his choices, his job and other demands, the man had lost his marriage, his kids, and his health. People were clapping, but his soul was dying.

If you achieved every goal you're chasing, would you be fulfilled? Or would it kill you?

The Solution

Have you ever heard of something called "reverse planning"? Until a few years ago, it was a concept that I knew very little about. But since then, it's become something I think about almost every day.

Reverse planning is starting with the "end" in mind. It's pausing today and thinking about where you want to be in ten, twenty, even fifty years from now. What is your goal? What are you chasing?

When we start with the end goal in mind, it allows us to reverse-plan our lives. What does getting *there* require of me this year, this month, this week, or even today? This exercise is extremely helpful for setting plans to accomplish your goals, but it is just as helpful in analyzing if your goals are worth pursuing.

What will this goal require of me? Do I like who I'll have to become to meet the goal? Is it going to be worth it?

So many people in our world today are chasing the end of rainbows that don't have a pot of gold waiting for them, but just a pot of emptiness, regret, and disappointment.

Jesus once said this: "What good is it for someone to gain the whole world, yet forfeit their soul?" (Mark 8:36). Beneath most people's goals lies a pursuit of the world. The solution to having the wrong goals is a simple one: have the right goals. More specifically, we have to pursue the right kingdom.

Jesus tells us, "But seek first *his kingdom* and his righteousness, and all these things will be given to you as well" (Matthew 6:33, emphasis added).

Chase those things that will last. Chase the right goals and you'll end up in the right place. Worldly goals lead to weak, ineffective Christians. Kingdom goals lead to powerful, purposeful, and fulfilled Christians.

Next Step Today

Stop and do a self-audit of your goals.

What are you chasing? Ask yourself honestly: are these goals worth pursuing? Are they going to give me what I think they'll give me?

I encourage you to write new goals for yourself that fit these requirements:

- Goals that build God's kingdom instead of yours.
- Goals that are tied to your purpose, not the accumulation of stuff.
- Goals that will have an eternal impact instead of a temporary one.
- Goals that help others instead of just helping yourself.

Here's an example of what my goals used to look like:

The goal is to make enough money to retire early.
To own a classic Ford Bronco.
To become the best sports broadcaster of all time.
To write a *New York Times* bestseller.
To live in a huge house with a pool and have a horse.

Here is what my goals look like now:

The goal is to be more in love with Jesus when I'm eighty than I am right now.
To celebrate our seventy-five-year wedding anniversary.
To raise kids who love the Lord.
To help people see how much Jesus loves them.
To have grandkids one day who love the Lord.
To become more generous this year than I was last year.
To make heaven as crowded as possible.
To be obedient with everything God asks of me.
To remain faithful to Jesus. Nothing more, and nothing less.

Take thirty minutes and reflect on your goals. Scratch the ones off the list that are killing you. Write down new ones that are going to give you life. Chase the right goals.

Habit to Work Toward

On Sunday nights, get into the habit of reflecting on your week.

How did you spend your time? Did your calendar match your new goals? If not, what do you need to change in the coming week regarding what you think about, what you work on, and what you prioritize?

One of my favorite adages is, "When you fail to plan, you plan to fail." That is true when it comes to our goals.

Truth to Believe

When I chase the right goals, it will lead to more purpose, fulfillment, and joy than I could possibly hope to experience by chasing the wrong goals.

4_

don't waste your life

The Problem

The world is great at lulling us to sleep. I'm not just talking about spending too much time watching Netflix or taking too many "power naps" throughout the week. The world is lulling us to sleep in our callings!

I must have heard this a thousand different ways . . .

"I'll go all in for Jesus once I graduate school."
"I'll surrender to His will once I get married."
"I'll make more time for God when I have more money."

Here's the problem: delayed obedience is still disobedience.

Here's the bigger problem when you do that: you're wasting your life.

The Solution

Stop procrastinating giving God your "yes."

Psalm 90:12 says, "Teach us to number our days, that we may gain a heart of wisdom." In other words, teach us to realize that our time on this earth is shorter than we know, so that we will stop wasting so much of it and live a wise and obedient life for Jesus!

God doesn't want our excuses. He wants our obedience. Right *now*.

Hebrews 11:1 says, "Now faith is confidence in what we hope for and assurance about what we do not see." This is one of the most well-known verses in the Bible about faith. But notice how the word *now* comes before the word *faith* in the verse: "Now faith . . ." The faith God wants you to have is not a "tomorrow" faith; it's a "right now" faith.

I'm not waiting to obey God—I'm doing it now.

I'm not waiting till I get the job I want—I'm making time now.

I'm not waiting till I get married—I'm surrendering now.

I'm not waiting till someone gives me permission—I'm obeying right now.

Your life doesn't start in the next season; it starts the moment you realize that Jesus is your prize, and He has called you to do great things today!

So wake up! Make your life count.

Say yes to Jesus today. Then wake up again tomorrow and do the same thing. Before you know it, you will look back and see that God can do the biggest things through our small, daily yeses.

Obedient lives start with obedient days. You can have one of those right *now*.

Next Step Today

The easiest person to lie to is yourself.

If you want to make the most of your life and your calling, it's going to require brutal honesty with yourself. What things have you been telling yourself you don't have time to do? What areas of your calling have you been avoiding and rationalizing in your mind?

It's time to address these lies and take a small step of obedience.

Shortly after following Jesus, I felt like God was calling me to be a pastor. That was a hilarious and scary thought to me. Me? A pastor? *Not of any church real people would go to*, I thought! I didn't have any formal training, and I was a brand-new Christian.

Though I had no idea how to become a pastor, I knew I wanted to be one someday.

Then one Sunday at church, I was smacked with the idea that I should start a Bible study. After a few minutes of thinking about it, I quickly changed my mind. A Bible study? That's cute. Maybe when I'm not a senior in college, juggling school and a job, and trying to figure out how to become a pastor. I had bigger things to think about.

For four straight months the thought of starting a Bible study would hit me at some point during the day, and every time I would push the idea away.

Finally, I relented. I sent a text to nine people and invited them to my small apartment to read the Bible together.

That Bible study that started with nine people met every week for the next five years and eventually turned into a college ministry with over seven hundred students. That Bible study led to a church hiring me as a college pastor.

I didn't have to know how to become a pastor. I didn't have to know how my calling would play out. I just had to be obedient today.

Habit to Work Toward

Track your excuses.

If you regularly find yourself feeling something in your soul that aligns with God's Word, but your immediate next thought is an excuse, this should be like an alarm going off: God might just be in this!

Write down what God is asking you to do. Pray about your excuses. Are they really reasons to wait, or do you need to obey?

Truth to Believe

God hasn't called me to a "one day" faith, but a "right now" faith. He can use me right where I am today!

5_

friends

The Problem

We severely underestimate the power that our friends have in our lives.

So many men go through life completely unaware of the influence their friends have on what they believe, the way they think and act. The idea that our friends don't determine much about our lives is a lie.

First Corinthians 15:33 says, "Bad company corrupts good character." The truth is that if you showed me your five closest friends, I would be able to show you your future.

There are very few decisions as important as deciding who will be our friends. Choose them wisely.

The Solution

When God really wants to bless you, He sends you a friend.

When it was time for David to become king, God didn't send him money, an army, power, or fame. He sent him a friend: Jonathan.

So when God wants to bless you, He sends you a friend. Likewise, when the devil wants to come after you, he will often send you a friend as well. It's up to you to discern whether it's God or the devil sending you the friend.

To start, you need friends who are secure enough to celebrate your successes as if they were their own. You need friends who are secure enough to call you out if your success ever gets to your head. You need friends who care more about who you are becoming than what you do. You need friends who will challenge you as a person of character and in what you do. You need friends who love Jesus more than anything else.

When I look back on the worst decisions I've made in my life, it's no coincidence that when I made those decisions, I simultaneously was surrounded by friends who did not push me to become more like Jesus. On the flip side of that, some of the best decisions I've ever made came because of the counsel and encouragement of godly friends.

I'm not saying all your friends need to be Christians. I believe that if we don't have friends who don't know the Lord, then there's probably a good chance we're not following the example of Jesus, since one of His nicknames was "friend of sinners."

But our closest friends, our "circle," need to look like Jesus. If bad company corrupts good character, then imagine what good company could do!

I've never had a better group of friends than I do right now. It has taken time, intentionality, and a whole lot of prayer. This has also been the sweetest season of my life. I have men of God around me who I get to learn from, lean on, and run through life's obstacles with.

Who are you running with?

Next Step Today

Check your circle.

Set aside time today to do a "friend audit." Which five friends do you spend the most time with and give the most priority to in your life? Do they make you want to be a better person? Do they make you more like Christ?

If the answer is yes—praise God! Now's the time to keep leaning into those friendships and make sure you're being the friend that they are to you.

If the answer is no, now might be the time to start creating a little distance between you and some of those friends. Again, it doesn't mean you can't be their friend. It just means you probably shouldn't be their best friend. You've got to protect that circle!

It's time to go friend-hunting.

Who are the people who have the same goals that you do as a man, those you also enjoy being around, spending time with? Now's the time to start thinking about how you can develop friendships with those people.

Check your circle → Change your circle → Be changed by your circle

Habit to Work Toward

For your friendships to have the greatest effect possible on your life, you've got to be a good friend as well.

Make a regular habit of checking in on your friends. Whether that's a weekly text, a phone call, or a time to get together and just talk, healthy friendships require regular communication.

Truth to Believe

A good and godly friend is worth more to me than gold.

6_

own your spiritual growth

The Problem

Imagine someone stocks your kitchen with all of your favorite foods—meats, fruits, veggies, breads, snacks, and of course Reese's Peanut Butter Cups.

Now imagine, three days later, the person who gave you the food calls you and asks how you're doing, and you say, "Man, I'm *starving*! I haven't eaten in days. I need someone to feed me."

They would probably respond, "What? Get up and eat!"

This is the situation so many men find themselves in spiritually. God has given us a book full of spiritual food (the Bible), which collects dust on the shelf while our spirits starve.

The Solution

Get up and eat.

Your spiritual growth is not someone else's job. It's yours!

Men don't wait around for someone else to feed them. Only children do that.

Men know where the food is, and they go and get it. Men eat regularly because they know that if they don't, it's only a matter of time before their lack of fuel causes them to slow down.

Your pastor can help you grow spiritually, but it is not his job. Your friends can help you grow spiritually, but it is not their job. Your family can help you grow spiritually, but it is not their job. Your spiritual growth is your own responsibility.

If you want to become more like Jesus, it's not going to happen by accident. It needs to happen intentionally and because *you* want it to.

One of the best ways to own your growth in Christ is to develop the right habits. These habits are important for everyone, but especially for men who aim to follow Christ. When you're born you look like your parents, but when you die you look like your habits. Don't like the way your life looks right now? If not, the first thing you should consider looking at is your habits.

Just as sinful habits lead to a sinful life, holy habits lead to a holy life. If you want to grow and mature in Him, you must put in place regular rhythms of being with Jesus, becoming like Him, and doing what He does.

Do you have habits that involve Jesus? It's impossible to regularly spend time with Jesus and not become more like Him. Protect your time with Him. Protect the time you spend seeking Him in His Word. Protect your time at the dinner table. EAT!

Next Step Today

Create a "meal plan."

When top-level athletes are training for a competition, they often follow a strict meal plan, including foods that will maximize their bodies' performance and output. They take the time to plan out every single thing they're going to put into their bodies and when they are going to eat it.

In 2 Timothy, Paul uses the illustration of an athlete to describe how we should approach following Jesus. In 1 Corinthians 9:26, Paul says, "Therefore I do not run like someone running aimlessly. . . ." In other words, we should approach our spiritual growth the way an athlete approaches their physical growth—with a plan! More specifically, we need a Bible-reading plan.

What kind of plan should you have? The best plan is the one you're likely to follow.

If you aren't currently reading your Bible at all right now, don't make a plan to read twenty-five chapters a day. There's no way you'll stick with it! It's too much too fast. Instead, make a plan that feels challenging enough to require something from you but easy enough that you will stick with it.

When I first started reading my Bible, I would read one chapter a day from the book of Proverbs and one chapter a day from the book of John. It was a great place to start.

It doesn't matter that much where you start. The point is just to start! Start eating today with intention and with a desire to get the most out of it spiritually as you run the race God has set before you.

Habit to Work Toward

Read your Bible for twenty to thirty minutes a day. If you consistently spend this much time in the Word each day while following a Bible-reading plan, you will easily read the entire Bible in a year.

I've found that the more I am in the Word, the more the Word gets in me.

Truth to Believe

My spiritual growth is my responsibility and no one else's. I'm going to grow in Christ because I want to, and I'm making a plan to do it.

7_

your phone lies

The Problem

The apple in the book of Genesis was used to deceive Adam and Eve in the Garden of Eden. The "apple" in your pocket today is being used to deceive you as well.

Our phones tell us it's normal to spend six-plus hours a day scrolling.

Our phones tell us liking a photo is the same thing as living in community.

Our phones tell us we can live our lives while simultaneously keeping up with the whole world.

Our phones promise a lot, but they take way more.

According to the World Happiness Report (yes, that's a real study), people have grown less and less happy since smartphones were introduced into society.

Our phones are lying to us.

The Solution

Use your phone, but don't let your phone use you.

Contrary to what you might think, I'm not some anti-technology purist who is here to tell you to destroy your phone.

(However, if your phone is destroying you, it might be worth it!) I'm fascinated by these small devices that have changed the modern world, and I think, when used correctly, they can do a lot of good.

However, I am here to say that if you don't set up guardrails for how you use your phone, and use it intentionally, your phone is likely to take so much more from your life than it will give.

The solution, then, is to use your phone intentionally and stop letting it use you subconsciously.

Imagine how good your soul would feel if instead of waking up using your phone as your alarm clock and then proceeding to check all your social-media accounts to start your day, you used an old-school alarm clock and didn't look at your phone until you had started the day reading your Bible?

Imagine how much more time you'd have if you set aside certain moments in your day to check your phone instead of letting the next push notification distract you from the people or important tasks in front of you?

Imagine how much deeper your relationships would be if you exchanged some of the text messages for in-person hangouts?

Imagine how much closer to God you could be if you shaved off just an hour a day of screen time and used that hour to pray, read your Bible, or worship?

If you can't give it up, it's probably got a hold on you. That's what it means to have an idol: something or someone that promises you the world and then requires a sacrifice.

Don't bow to your phone. Instead, turn to Him, to more in-person community—more living, more contentment, more joy. More falling in love with God.

Next Step Today

Your next step is to buy an alarm clock.

Seriously. I promise you it will change your life.

welcome to manhood

For a long time I used my phone as my alarm and didn't think twice about it. It would ring early in the morning, I'd stretch my arm over, unplug it and immediately catch up on any texts, emails, or social-media posts I'd missed while catching some Z's.

The problem was that I was letting the urgent yet unimportant things keep me from the life-giving, most important thing in my life: God.

Rather than spend the first fifteen to twenty minutes of my day doing stuff I could do another time, I choose to spend these minutes with God. If we spend the first fifteen to twenty minutes of each day on social media, we're apt to see/read things that will plant unhealthy thoughts of comparison, greed, lust, or worse into our minds when instead we could be focused on God's Word, filling our thoughts with His truth.

So your next step is to stop letting your phone take your mornings from you!

I use my watch as an alarm now. It doesn't show texts or notifications. It simply tells the time and beeps at me when I need to get up. It's the best.

If you don't have a watch, there are tons of really cool and cheap alarm clocks you can find online. Get one today! And start charging your phone in your kitchen or living room.

Begin your day with peace, love, joy, and a sound mind instead of with the anxiety, busyness, comparison, and discontentment our phones so often throw at us.

Make a deal with yourself that you aren't going to talk to the world until you've first talked to God.

Habit to Work Toward

Once you get your new morning routine down, take it a step further: set up times in the day when you will check social media and then make those apps off-limits the rest of the day.

Instead of social media being an ongoing conversation between you and your phone, let it be a once or twice a day check-in. It only feels like you're missing out until you realize how much life you've been missing out on by refreshing your newsfeed every few minutes.

Truth to Believe

I will not miss out on the life I want to live because I'm too busy keeping up with everyone else's.

8_

selfishness

The Problem

When I visited Israel, I got to swim in the Dead Sea. Our tour guide told us that one of the reasons it's called the "dead" sea is because it receives water from multiple other sources of water, but it does not give up water anywhere else. Scientifically, this kills life.

Because the sea receives but never gives, it's become dead.

When we receive and don't give, our soul does the same thing: it dies.

We live in a world that loves to receive, yet we follow a man named Jesus who loved to give and commanded us to do the same.

The Solution

Biblically, it's clear that there's a way of life that leads to emptiness, pain, and regret. It's living life believing that your time, talents, and treasure are all about you, and all for you. It's approaching situations asking the question, What can I get out of this?

selfishness

But there's another way of life that leads to fulfillment, purpose, and freedom. Jesus talks about this in the book of Luke:

> Give away your life; you'll find life given back, but not merely given back—given back with bonus and blessing. Giving, not getting, is the way. Generosity begets generosity.
>
> Luke 6:38 (MSG)

If you want a blessed life, the way to realize it is not by getting, but by giving. Live your life with the understanding that your time, talents, and treasure are not for you but for the benefit of others and, more importantly, for the glory of God!

What's mind-blowing is that when we live life Jesus' way, He promises to pour out even more blessing on us. In Luke 16:10, Jesus says, "Whoever can be trusted with very little can also be trusted with much." In other words, when we pour back out what Jesus has given us, it leads to God trusting us with even more. Sometimes the more God trusts us with is greater opportunity. Other times God pours out more of other things such as joy, peace, and hope.

There's a man who attends our church who I believe is genuinely one of the happiest people on the planet. He's the kind of guy who instantly makes every room lighter, warmer, more at ease. His laugh is infectious. Others want him around as much as possible because his energy and love of life draw them in and make them feel special.

Over the last year or so, I've learned a lot about this man. He's not wealthy but works a regular nine-to-five job, and his life appears very normal—that is, with the exception of one small thing: he's obsessed with serving others.

He spends his Sundays serving all day at our church. During the week he serves regularly at a food ministry that feeds people experiencing poverty. It seems he is always the first one to respond when someone needs help. He's a walking HELP to others.

If you want a full and enriching life, stop making your life about you and instead make it about others. Give!

Next Step Today

If you don't have a regular time in your week that's focused on serving other people, now is the time to do it. One of the best and easiest places to start is to serve at a local church.

As a pastor, I've watched time and time again how serving at church can change lives. It doesn't just change the lives of the people who are served; it changes the lives of those who are serving.

One night at our church we hosted a celebration for the hundreds of people who serve there. It was one of the most powerful things I've ever been a part of. Person after person shared how God had radically changed their lives, not once they started attending our church but once they started *serving* at church! As these people gave up their Sunday mornings to serve, they began to experience breakthroughs in their personal lives, find community they had never found before, and see God use them directly in helping others find Him for themselves.

What more could you want than that? Sign me up!

Serving at a local church doesn't require that you be the most talented; it just requires that you be available. Your pastor will be grateful if you do it, yet I promise that one day you'll be even more grateful you did it than they are.

Habit to Work Toward

We all need a place to serve regularly, but we also all need a place to serve that's outside of our comfort zones.

selfishness

One or two times a year, where could you serve that would require you to take a step of faith? Maybe it's on a missions trip overseas. Maybe it's somewhere down the street that needs your help. I've learned that when I step out of my comfort zone to serve others, the Holy Spirit becomes my comforter and helps me serve others and do what's needed.

Truth to Believe

I'm never more like Jesus than when I serve others out of love.

9_

stop playing it safe

The Problem

So many people miss seeing God move because of this:

Everything they do, everything they pray for, and everything they're believing and hoping for could happen without God having to show up.

We serve a God who loves us and who loves to do the impossible. We've been given a winning hand and yet we are still playing it safe.

Stop. Playing. It. Safe.

The Solution

God hasn't called us to settle for normal lives. He hasn't called us to play it safe. He hasn't called us even to do hard things. No, He's called us to do impossible things!

Jesus' own words pointed to this truth when He said, "Very truly I tell you, whoever believes in me will do the works I have been doing, and they will do even greater things than these, because I am going to the Father" (John 14:12).

That verse confused me for a long time. I've never healed the blind or the sick. I've never raised anyone from the dead. I've never turned fish sticks and toast into a buffet for thousands of people. Does Jesus know how average I am?

And yet Jesus meant what He said. We *can* do impossible things. However, this requires (a) that we believe in and fully rely on God; and (b) that we have faith to try impossible things.

Faith and playing it safe cannot coexist.

God loves to call His people to the impossible because the impossible requires that we stop depending on our talents, work ethic, strategies, and resources and start depending fully on Him. This has been God's desire all along, that you would turn to Him first and no one/nothing else.

He also calls us to the impossible because only He can get the glory from that. When you do something hard, people can give you the glory for it. But when you do something impossible, people know you couldn't have done it by yourself, and they suddenly become curious about how it happened!

"Hey, tell me more about that. How in the world . . . ?"

And this provides the opportunity for you to answer and boldly give the glory to God and to Him alone.

David wasn't playing it safe when he stepped onto the battlefield to face Goliath.

Moses wasn't playing it safe when he led the Israelites out of captivity.

Gideon wasn't playing it safe with a company of 300 soldiers, facing down an enemy consisting of 120,000.

Paul wasn't playing it safe when he worshiped while in prison.

All of them stepped out in faith, and God, faithful to His Word, showed up to bring about the impossible through them.

In what ways are you playing it safe right now?

The solution is to live a life only God could get the credit for. Ask God for those things only He could give or do. Ask God to use you in ways that would require Him to have to show up.

Stop. Playing. It. Safe.

Next Step Today

Do a risk assessment.

Take a few moments today and reflect on these questions:

1. Is there any part of my life that requires God to show up, otherwise _____ will not happen or succeed?
2. Do I have to depend on God for anything, or is my life fully dependent on me?

If you assess your life and realize you're playing it safe, then dig deeper. Is there a reason behind this, or has it just kind of worked out that way? Where has complacency or a lack of faith crept in? Is there some fear of failure or maybe a fear of people's opinions that is holding you back? Is it because you just don't know where or how to start fully depending on God?

It all begins with being honest. If we can't be real with ourselves, we can't better ourselves.

Habit to Work Toward

One habit that's changed my life is to write down my prayers.

At the end of my quiet time with God, I jot down things I'm praying for. There are many prayers that don't require a ton of faith. Prayers for a good dentist appointment with less pain than the last one; for it not to rain during an event we're hosting; or maybe something as small as my son not peeing his pants today (we're potty training currently).

But here I write down prayer requests that truly require an unwavering faith:

God, give our church a building in the middle of Nashville.

God, heal my friend of stage 4 cancer.

God, let us see 10,000 people give their lives to Jesus at our church.

God, save the guy from my high school who mocks Christians online.

This is one of the most faith-building things I've done in the last few years—writing down impossible prayers. I've been praying and looking back and seeing how God showed up, turning my requests from impossible to possible. I think this habit or practice will bless you too.

Truth to Believe

When I'm fully surrendered and fully dependent on God, He will do impossible things through me.

10_

stop following your heart

The Problem

There's a lot of bad advice out there. Some of the worst advice you'll hear today is to follow your heart.

This sounds great on the surface, yet it fleshes out horribly. The Bible doesn't tell us to follow our hearts; on the contrary, it teaches us to *beware* of our hearts: "The heart is deceitful above all things and beyond cure. Who can understand it?" (Jeremiah 17:9).

We want to believe our hearts have our best interests in mind, but in truth they're sick. They're full of sin, fleshly desires, and corruption. Following the heart has become a popular path for many, yet it's not the path for those of us who desire to reach a destination of peace, hope, and love.

The Solution

The problem with following one's heart is that our hearts are constantly changing. The solution is to follow Jesus, for He never changes.

stop following your heart

If I could go back in time ten years and ask my heart what it wanted, it would probably spit out a list that looks something like this:

- Jeans so skinny I can't breathe.
- To marry a girl named ___.
- To have a long and successful career in sports broadcasting.
- A large bowl of cookies-and-cream ice cream.

Fast-forward to today:

- I got rid of all my skinny jeans.
- I'm thankful God didn't let me marry the person I wanted to marry back then.
- I'm a pastor now and living my absolute dream.
- I still want a large bowl of cookies-and-cream ice cream, but I'm definitely lactose intolerant.

My point is that our hearts, our cravings, and our feelings are always changing. If we follow them, not only will we likely not end up where we want to go but we will have spiritual whiplash!

Proverbs 3:5 says, "Trust in the LORD with all your heart and lean not on your own understanding."

Let's be real—our own understanding is no understanding. We don't know what's best for us. We don't even know what's good for us. But God does, and He always "works for the good of those who love him, who have been called according to his purpose" (Romans 8:28).

Don't listen to your thoughts; listen to what the Bible says.
Don't be guided by your feelings; be guided by the Holy Spirit.

45

Don't chase what is popular right now; chase what is true forever.

Don't follow your heart; follow Jesus.

Next Step Today

I've found that most big decisions in life fall under one of five different categories:

1. Spiritual
2. Family
3. Friends
4. Work
5. Dreams

Go through each of these categories today and figure out which ones have you following your heart instead of following Jesus. Is there a category or two where you're trying to force your will instead of God's? Is there anywhere you're constantly flip-flopping or are confused about? If so, there's a good chance you need to submit it to God.

Stop playing tug-of-war with God over who's leading your life. Take the rope of control, tie it around the cross, and tell God, "Your kingdom come, your will be done. I'm following you."

Habit to Work Toward

"What does the Bible say about this?"

This is one of my favorite questions to ask. When things happen, or you're presented with a fork in the road, make a habit of asking this question and finding out the answer.

So much heartache and regret could be avoided if we just slowed down long enough to learn what God's Word says before making a decision.

Truth to Believe

I can't trust my heart because it is deceitful. But I can trust Jesus and His Word because He always has my best interests in mind.

11_

lust

The Problem

Too many men are losing the fight against lust.

According to Springer's Sexuality Research in 2022, roughly 84 percent of males ages 16–30 look at pornography at least one time per month.

Too many young men are lying to themselves by saying they will stop this habit once they get married.

Too many young men are letting their cravings change their identities.

Too many young men are rationalizing their sin.

Too many young men don't know how to win the fight against lust.

The Solution

First off, what exactly is lust?

The lust I'm talking about in this chapter is the sexual kind. It's any kind of sexual desire or temptation that, when acted upon, leads to sin. God has a beautiful and specific design for sex. Lust is the participation in anything sexual outside of that design.

We live in a world that says lust and love are one and the same. That our sexual desires should be king of our lives, and that if we follow what it is they want, we will be happy. This is a lie. Lust and love lead to two very different realities:

Lust says, "I want you." Love says, "I want what's best for you."

Lust says, "What can you do for me?" Love says, "What can I do for you?"

Lust is short-lived, while love plays the long game. Lust moves quickly. Love is patient.

Lust is about me. Love is about someone else. Lust is self-serving. Love is selfless. Lust ends in destruction. Love leads to joy and contentment.

Are you in lust, or are you in love?

If you're one of the many who struggle with sexual temptation, I've got good news for you: you can overcome it with the help of the Holy Spirit.

The first step in winning the fight against lust is not to try to fight it. Freedom is found in *fleeing* from it.

"Flee from sexual immorality. All other sins a person commits are outside the body, but whoever sins sexually, sins against their own body" (1 Corinthians 6:18). Not only does this Scripture warn us of the consequences of sexual sin but it gives us the starting place for defeating it: RUN!

In Genesis 39, a young man named Joseph finds himself in a tricky situation. He is alone with his boss's wife, and she makes a move on him, attempting to get him to sleep with her. He doesn't stop to try to talk her out of it. He doesn't begin to explain why it would be wrong. He doesn't even quote Scripture to her. Instead, he runs!

There are many ways we can stand and fight sin. But when it comes to sexual sin, we need to learn to run away from it. We are weak. If we stay too close to it, eventually we'll participate in it.

We flee from lust by removing ourselves from those areas where we could be tempted by lust.

Flee by charging your phone and laptop in another room, not your bedroom. Flee by giving other people access to your social-media accounts. Flee by unfollowing thirst traps. Flee by not hanging out with your girlfriend alone at night.

If you're losing the fight to lust and want to win, then start fleeing.

Next Step Today

Sexual sin is most effective in the dark, which means we need to drag it out into the light.

Ephesians 5:13 says, "But everything exposed by the light becomes visible—and everything that is illuminated becomes a light."

We drag our struggles into the light in two primary ways:

1. We repent. We tell God about it and ask for His forgiveness as we intentionally turn away from what we did and turn toward Jesus and the life He has for us.
2. We tell others.

You need help in this fight, and the Bible is clear that when we invite others into our journey to overcome sin, it works!

James 5:16 says, "Therefore confess your sins to each other and pray for each other so that you may be healed." We confess to God to receive forgiveness of our sin. We confess to others to be healed from our sin.

When we drag our sin into the light and let the right people know that we need help, it exposes what has been in the dark and helps us find freedom against that sin.

Who do you need to confess to today besides Jesus? It could be a pastor, a parent, a mentor, or a really good friend. Stop fighting in the shadows today and step into the light.

Habit to Work Toward

Form an accountability group or partnership with people who desire God's plan for their sexual life like you do.

Download the Covenant Eyes app on your phones together. This screen-accountability software gives other people access to what you've been looking at and helps drag temptation into the light. Commit to praying with one another and for one another. If anyone stumbles, be there to encourage each other and press forward.

Check in once a week and see how things are going. One of the best ways to walk in holiness in this area is to do so with a group you trust.

Truth to Believe

I don't have to give in to sexual sin because I'm an overcomer through Christ Jesus.

12_

servants > leaders

The Problem

We have a twisted view of leadership.

Today, even among Christians, it seems there's an obsession with leadership. How do we become better leaders? How do we make more leaders? What leadership content can we consume?

I love leadership. Truly I do. I listen to leadership podcasts and want to be the best leader I can be. My concern is that we are too concerned with something that Jesus was clearly not concerned with. I'm worried that we're trying to climb a ladder that Jesus was, through His actions and example, climbing down.

The Bible mentions the word *leadership* just six times, but it refers to the word *servant* a total of 1,100 times.

The problem is that we care more about being leaders than about being servants.

The Solution

Become a servant.

When people say the word *leader* in Christian spaces, I think it's important to qualify that servant leadership is biblical leadership.

You can be a "great leader" and not look like Jesus. But it's much harder to be a great servant and not look like Jesus. Jesus is looking for servants.

Leadership today promotes distance. Servant leadership requires proximity. Leadership today is often me-focused. Servant leadership is others-focused. Leadership today doesn't care for messy people or situations. Servant leadership moves right toward them. Leadership today is about becoming more. Servant leadership is about becoming less.

I love this quote by Henri Nouwen:

> Too often I looked at relevance, popularity and power as ingredients of leading an effective ministry. The truth, however, is that these are not celebrations but temptations.

There is some part inside all of us that desires the admiration of others. Who doesn't want to be seen as a great leader? Who doesn't want people to think they are impressive?

Jesus would call those desires prideful.

But there's a healthy side of leadership, and this healthy side comes from having pure motives. Motives to help people, improve their lives, and see others thrive. These things only happen when we desire to serve others more than we desire to lead others.

In the kingdom of God, if you are too big to serve, then you are too small to lead. But when you spend your life pouring into and serving others, with no ulterior motives, you'll look up one day and realize that people are following you. Not because you're some amazing person, but because you followed Jesus and His playbook of what true leadership is.

Think about it. Jesus didn't hoard up; He gave away. Jesus didn't write a book on leadership; He washed others' feet. Jesus didn't help himself; He helped those around Him. Jesus didn't "climb the ladder" for himself; He climbed the cross to rescue us.

If you want to lead, follow Jesus. Serve.

Next Step Today

Ask yourself this simple question: "In what ways am I taking instead of giving?"

One of my favorite leadership quotes is one by John Maxwell about serving: "We make a living by what we get, but we make a life by what we give."

What's one area in your life today where you could flip the switch from receiving to giving? What's one act you could do that would show someone in your life that you're there to serve them?

A life of serving others starts with making it a habit to serve others. A habit of serving others starts with the decision to serve one person today.

Who could you serve today?

Habit to Work Toward

My dad refuses to eat until everyone else has made themselves up a plate of food. Since I was a little kid, whether at family gatherings, work outings, wherever we are, not one time have I seen my dad not go to the back of the food line.

This may seem like a small thing, but it has made a huge impact on me. My dad gets it: servants go last. Jesus said as much when talking about His kingdom: "But many who are first will be last, and many who are last will be first" (Matthew 19:30).

Try building the habit of going last. In the buffet line, through the door, at the four-way stop in your car, at the airport security line. Leaders go first, but servants go last.

Truth to Believe

If I want to lead like Jesus, I must serve like Jesus.

13_
dating

The Problem

We don't know how to date anymore.

Yeah, I said the quiet part out loud. We don't know how to date! And by "we," I'm talking about Christian men.

We've let loneliness lower our standards. We get into relationships with no clear intentions. We date based on potential instead of prayer. We get into relationships too quickly, and we take too long to get out of the wrong ones.

We all want a great marriage one day, but we fail to realize that the foundation of a great marriage is built during the dating season.

We can date better.

The Solution

Let me preface what I'm about to lay out for you in this chapter with this: my dating thoughts are pretty intense. And by that I mean *intensely* different from how the world tells you to date.

Until I'd started dating my now-wife, my dating season was a shambles. I messed it up about as badly as anybody could mess it up. I'm sharing this from the experience of someone who dated poorly, but who eventually dated well. You don't have to follow my advice here, but if you'd like to save yourself from some regret, heartache, and possibly even sin, I invite you to keep reading.

1. Don't date "potential."
   Potential is a nice thing to notice, but it's a horrible thing to date. There's a chance that the potential you see in someone grows and turns into reality. Yet the problem with potential is that there's also the possibility they *never* become the person you thought they would be someday. You might date potential and then marry potential only for that potential never to materialize, and "till death do us part" is a long time to be wrong.

   Instead of dating potential, date the proof of concept.

   Date someone who already loves Jesus. Date someone who already finds their identity in Christ. Date someone who already is kind to others. Date someone who is already transparent. Date someone who serves God now.

2. Don't date until you can see yourself getting married in the next year.
   I told you—this is intense advice. I'm well aware that multiyear dating relationships prior to marriage are quite popular. I'm also aware that most of them include having sexual relations before marriage. Which do you care about more? Your relationship status or your holiness before God?

   If you're in an inappropriate relationship right now, my advice would be to seriously pray about stepping out of it for a season until you can date God's way. If you're not in a relationship at the moment, then I'd suggest you pray about staying out of one until you can seriously see yourself getting married to the woman God has for you within a year's time. When we put intentional parameters around the dating season, this helps in keeping the relationship healthy, moving toward marriage and all that's holy.

3. Don't hang out with your dating partner alone at night. I'm sure there are men who can do this consistently over time and not stumble into sin; I just haven't met any of them yet.

4. Be slow to date, but quick to break up.
Take your time getting into a relationship. Be sure of their character first. If at any moment you don't believe they could be your spouse, *break up*. Anything less is wasting and dishonoring both their time and yours. Make sure you spend time with them in the most important areas of life: at church, in mixed company, with family, and with friends.

Next Step Today

I've found that a lot of men struggle with choosing the right person to date because they've never prayed about the right person to date. If you don't know who/what you're looking for, how can you expect to recognize and know it when they show up?

I'd encourage you to sit down and make a list of traits you're praying for in a future spouse. After a few years of being single and dating, that's exactly what I did. My list looked like this:

I pray that . . .

Her character would be her most attractive quality.
She would laugh a lot.
She would find her validation in Jesus and not in others or even me.
She would love doing ministry and serving others.

She'd be a dreamer.

She'd treat people well, who couldn't give her anything in return.

She'd be someone I could have fun doing anything with.

She'd have the desire to start a family one day.

These are just some of the things on my list I was praying for. The main point is this: you should pray for your future spouse.

Talk to God about your dating life. He cares more than you realize! He might even help more than you realize. He definitely did so for me.

Habit to Work Toward

If you find yourself single or dating, the time to start praying for your future spouse is right now.

Don't wait to sow or invest in your future marriage. It doesn't have to be long prayers or even everyday prayers. But you should regularly talk to God about one of the most important decisions you will ever make.

Truth to Believe

I'm a son of God, and it's possible for me to live a holy life that is pleasing to Him in my dating relationships.

14_

relationship or religion?

The Problem

"Relationship is greater than religion."

About a decade ago that phrase become extremely popular in Christian circles. Pastors began applying these five words in their sermons, it inspired entire books from Christian authors, and it caught on culturally so much that believers across different age groups began quoting the phrase.

The quote became popular because it's true.

What's the problem, then?

The problem is that many Christians began using the quote as an excuse for not putting any effort into their relationship with Jesus.

No time spent with God? No Bible reading? No prayer? No becoming more like Jesus? It's fine because "relationship is greater than religion"!

The Solution

Imagine if I said I wanted a great marriage but was unwilling to talk to my wife. Imagine if I said I wanted our marriage to be amazing but refused to go on dates, spend time with, or even be around my wife. You'd say I was crazy!

Because the truth is this: great relationships require effort. If you want your relationship with Jesus to be all that it can be, that's going to require effort as well.

Now, before you freak out, I am NOT saying your relationship with Jesus is earned by your effort. I'm simply saying it's developed through effort. We're not talking about what gets you into heaven. No, what we're talking about is what gets heaven into you!

Dallas Willard said it best: "Grace is not opposed to effort. It is opposed to earning. Earning is an attitude. Effort is an action." A relationship with Jesus is so much greater than rules or religion. Which is exactly why our relationship with Him is worth the effort.

So many Christians see spiritual disciplines or spiritual habits as rules they must follow instead of what they really are—ways to sow/invest in their relationship with Jesus.

The solution: we have to switch our perspective. I don't have to read my Bible or pray or fast or sit in silence with the Lord. I get to do those things; I get to spend time with God! I get to talk to Him! I get to be in relationship with the God of the universe, and He knows me by name.

When we approach our time with Jesus with that perspective, truly a relationship becomes greater than religion.

Next Step Today

Today is a great day to simply remind yourself of the miracle of your relationship with Jesus.

Take a few minutes to think about all that had to happen just for you to be able to have a relationship with the Lord. God had to send His only Son down to earth to be with us. That Son, Jesus, lived thirty-three years without ever sinning or falling short even once. After living a perfect life, He was executed on a cross, taking on himself the punishment for all your sins. Three days after dying for you, He rose from the dead for you! Proving once and for all that sin, death, Satan, and hell were defeated. Finally, the chasm between a sinful humanity was bridged because of the payment for sins that Jesus paid.

"God made him who had no sin to be sin for us, so that in him we might become the righteousness of God" (2 Corinthians 5:21).

When we reflect on the miracle of how our relationship with Jesus came to be, this keeps us from taking it for granted.

Jesus wanted a relationship with us so deeply that He was willing to pay for it with His life. As we come face-to-face with this reality, then putting effort into the relationship is something we long to give.

Habit to Work Toward

Put effort in your relationship with Jesus—every day! Start with just ten minutes. How can you spend ten minutes per day with Jesus? Is it in prayer? Is it in reading your Bible? Is it in listening to a podcast or sermon that helps you reflect on Him? Set aside ten minutes per day, and what once felt like a duty to you will eventually feel like a delight.

Truth to Believe

My relationship with Jesus is the most beautiful thing in my life, and it's worth my effort and focused attention.

15_

the bible

The Problem

It's hard to follow Jesus if you don't know who He is and what it was He said.

The Bible is God's Word, but the problem is we don't read and study it like we should. According to research done by the Pew Research Center in 2024, only 9 percent of Christians read their Bibles multiple times a week!

And yet without the Bible serving as the compass in our lives, we will surely fall prey to all sorts of attacks from our very real enemy, Satan.

The Solution

I suffer from horrible tree and pollen allergies, as in I'm straight-up allergic to the outdoors! Which is tough right now because it's early spring in Nashville as I'm writing this.

Last week I cut the grass, and I guess something was blooming extra ferociously, for within an hour of finishing the yard work my eyes had turned red, my nose stuffy, and my face was swollen up as if I'd just gotten stung by an army of bees.

the bible

I immediately called my allergist for help, and the first thing he asked me was, "Have you been taking your allergy medicine?"

I told him I hadn't been, but that I took an allergy pill right after cutting the grass because I could feel my symptoms flaring up. He laughed and told me that's not how the medication works. The med must be in your system consistently for it to work.

The Bible works the same way in our lives. We need to know the Word before we need the Word!

If you wait until trials and temptations show up to start reading your Bible, you're going to be no match for those things. But if you spend time each day in the Word of God, little by little, God's Word begins to take residence in your heart. I like to say it this way: get in the Word, then watch God's Word get in you!

Psalm 119:11 says, "I have hidden your word in my heart that I might not sin against you." When you've hidden God's Word in your heart, and life gets hard, it will be the Word of God that sustains you. When life becomes confusing, it will be the Word of God that brings you clarity and truth. When life becomes discouraging, it will be the Word of God that brings you hope.

The solution is to spend a little bit of time in God's Word each day and let this practice do the good work God intends it to do.

Next Step Today

One of the easiest ways to get going in this area is to follow a Bible reading plan.

I'd highly recommend checking out the YouVersion Bible app. This app offers many different reading plans depending on a person's goal and season of life.

A lot of people have asked me where I would start if I had never read the Bible before, and the following books of the Bible are my go-to answer (this is just my personal preference):

John
Acts
James
Genesis

I'd also recommend reading one chapter per day from the book of Proverbs. Since there are thirty-one chapters in all, you can just read whatever chapter matches the day of the month and keep going like that. Proverbs is full of amazing wisdom, which is 100 percent applicable to our lives today.

What's the best Bible reading plan? The plan that you'll stick to!

I mentioned earlier that one of my favorite quotes is, "Those who fail to plan, plan to fail." I think the same is true with the Bible. Those who fail to plan for reading their Bible regularly, plan to fail reading their Bible.

So make a plan today, and start reading!

Habit to Work Toward

A great way to begin reading the Bible is to take notes using the SOAP method. SOAP stands for: Scripture, Observation, Application, Prayer.

Write out the Scripture verse or verses. List the observations you see in the text. Write down whatever applications you think you should be applied to your own life. Then pray about it.

Truth to Believe

The Bible is not just a book; it's God speaking to me. And I want to know what He has to say!

16_

comparison

The Problem

Many of us struggle with OCD—Obsessive Comparison Disorder.

With a smartphone constantly in our pockets, we're always seconds away from being tempted to compare our lives to someone else's. Comparison is a potentially devastating habit for men wanting to follow Jesus.

Because the fastest way to kill something special is to compare it with something else.

When we compare our calling, our progress, or our relationship with Jesus to other men's, what we're doing is taking for granted the unique things God has blessed us with! Comparison reveals that we are chasing gifts instead of the giver. Comparison proves that our eyes have shifted from being focused on Christ.

The Solution

Be confident in who you are, and comfortable with who you are not. How do you do this?

1. Recognize that you are God's workmanship.
   Psalm 139:14 says, "I praise you because I am fearfully and wonderfully made; your works are wonderful."

In other words, God designed you on purpose and for a purpose. When you stop believing the lies of the enemy and begin believing the truth about who God made you to be, you will stop wanting to live everybody else's life and start thanking God for your own!

You are wonderful. God had options, yet He chose you. Believe it!

2. Recognize you're on the same team.

Comparison causes you to treat teammates like enemies. In the kingdom of God, we are all on the same team. We shouldn't be jealous when one of our neighbors wins. We should celebrate because God is in the neighborhood!

It's not our kingdom; it's God's kingdom. It's not our neighbors' kingdom; it's God's kingdom. One of the fastest ways to end comparison in your life is to celebrate others, quickly and often.

3. Focus on obedience to God.

For so many people, success = competition. We feel successful when we compare what we do, or what we have, with others, and it looks "better." But that's not success at all. That's pride.

True success is not me compared to you. True success is me compared to what God has asked me to do. True success is obedience to God. If we want to be the men of God that He's called us to be, we need to keep our eyes off the scoreboard and on Jesus Christ.

Next Step Today

Who are you comparing yourself to?

Be honest. Who did your mind just jump to when you read that line?

comparison

I've found that if I can't celebrate someone, it's probably because I keep comparing myself to that person. Who is it you have a hard time celebrating? Usually it's not the people who do totally different things from you. It's the people who do the same things we do, and we are insecure about their ability to do them better.

What if I told you that you could experience overwhelming freedom today by simply reaching out to that person you've been comparing yourself to and paying them a genuine compliment?

So much freedom can be found in celebrating others.

For about a year I compared myself to another young pastor. The comparison was so deep in my heart that I rationalized the negative things I thought about him with all sorts of lies and garbage. The truth? He was just a great pastor, and I was insecure that he was better at it than me.

One day God convicted me and told me to call him. When he answered the phone, I immediately asked him for his forgiveness. I told him I had thought negative things about him over the last year that weren't true. That I had compared opportunities, ministry size, and sermons all because of my own issue with pride.

I asked for forgiveness and then I celebrated him.

I told him that he was a phenomenal pastor and preacher, a man worth emulating, and that from that day forward I wanted to be a friend and a good teammate in whatever way I could.

What shocked me was that he apologized for doing some of the same things I had done. We both experienced freedom that day through confession and celebration.

You may need to close this book for a few minutes. Is there someone you should call?

Habit to Work Toward

When you have thoughts of comparison about someone, stop what you are doing and celebrate them. Comment on their post. Send them a text. Call them and speak a blessing of life over them.

Cultivate the habit of killing comparison through celebrating others.

Truth to Believe

I don't have to compare or compete with others because God made me intentionally, and my calling is special.

17_

clarity or trust

The Problem

We want clarity too much.

I'm convinced that the most popular thing people pray for is clarity. We want clarity about our relationships. We want clarity about our careers. We want clarity about our callings.

Clarity isn't a bad thing. In fact, it can be great! It's just not how God works all the time.

God often gives us enough clarity for the next step, but very rarely does He give us clarity for the entire journey. Why? Because if we knew how everything was going to work out, we would trust our plans more than we trust Him!

The problem is we want clarity more than we want to trust God.

The Solution

Pray for a heart that trusts God completely.

The Israelites didn't have clarity in the wilderness; they had to trust. David didn't have clarity in Saul's throne room; he had to trust. The disciples didn't have clarity about the Holy Spirit; they had to trust.

Trust requires proximity, and God wants us to be close. It's fine to ask God for clarity. Just don't do it at the expense of trusting Him.

Proverbs 3:5–6 says, "Trust in the LORD with all your heart and lean not on your own understanding; in all your ways submit to him, and he will make your paths straight."

Here's the truth: we can stress about all that we don't know, or we can trust the God who promises to make our paths straight. One option comes with a lot of fear and anxiety, and the other option comes with His peace and blessing.

Here's another way to put it:

One of the greatest basketball players ever to step onto the court was a man named Michael Jordan. Now, if you gave me a basketball, I might shoot it at the wrong hoop. But the same basketball can be taken out of my hands and put into the hands of Michael Jordan, and it's instantly worth significantly more. Why? Because Michael knows what to do with it.

It's the same with my life, and the same with your life. My life in my hands is going to end up an absolute mess. But my life in the hands of Jesus is a completely different story. Why? Because He knows what to do with it!

Trust Him.

Next Step Today

The areas where you worry most show where you trust God the least.

For a few minutes today, think about where you worry the most. Is there some area or thing your mind naturally turns to throughout the day? Is there a part of your life that's giving you much anxiety? If so, this is a huge alarm that you might not be trusting God the way you should.

Here's a prayer to help with whatever it is you find yourself worrying about right now:

Lord Jesus, I pray today for trust. You are trustworthy. Not only are you trustworthy but you care for me. Your Word says in 1 Peter 5:7 that I can cast all my anxiety on you because you care for me. So that's what I do today. I cast _____ at your feet.

I don't want to keep trying to figure it all out on my own. I'd much rather let you take the wheel and follow where you lead me. Today I'm not asking for clarity. Instead, I'm asking that you give me the courage to trust you during the times I would normally worry. I want to be close to you, Jesus. I know that's the best place I can be. Amen.

Habit to Work Toward

When I'm worried, stressed, or anxious, the most helpful thing is to go on a "worship walk."

I put on my favorite worship playlist and go for a long walk. Sometimes I sing on the walk, sometimes I pray, and sometimes I just walk. It's a physical and spiritual exercise to stop trying to figure out what to do and instead draw close to the One who knows what to do.

Try it. You might just start trusting a little bit more each time you worship and walk.

Truth to Believe

I can trust Jesus with my life because there's no one more trustworthy than Him.

18_
ask bigger

The Problem

Our prayers are too small. We don't ask big enough!

Hebrews 11:6 says, "Without faith it is impossible to please God, because anyone who comes to him must believe that he exists and that he rewards those who earnestly seek him."

The two times in the Bible where Jesus expressed amazement was due to people having such big faith.

Our problem is that our prayers are so small that they reveal our lack of faith. If God answered every single thing you prayed for this morning, would it change the world? Would it even change your world?

The truth is that God loves it when we ask boldly in His name. We need to ask *bigger*.

The Solution

One Saturday morning, during a time when I was fundraising to start our new church, I took a businessman to breakfast to share with him our vision for the church in hopes of convincing him to invest financially in that vision. I asked the man for $5,000, which to me was a lot of money. To my shock, he didn't even hesitate and said yes. I was ecstatic!

About thirty minutes later, we were standing in the parking lot, preparing to say goodbye, when he asked me why I hadn't asked him for more money. I was confused.

He said, "You told me that to start this church, you were going to need a lot more than $5,000, so why did you ask me for only $5,000?"

I told him I just thought that amount was what he might consider giving. He laughed and said, "Well, Noah, I would have given you $20,000 today, but you didn't ask big enough. I'll give you the other $15,000 one day, but I'm only going to give you the $5,000 today because I want you to remember the time you didn't ask big."

You know what has been keeping me up at night? The thought that I'll get to heaven one day and hear God tell me, "I could have done more for you, Noah, but you never asked me."

We need to pray for more!

We need to pray for more people to find Jesus. We need to pray for more miracles. More church plants. More missionaries. More baptisms. More of God's kingdom on this earth!

The solution is we need to pray like we have the God of the universe on our side—because we do!

Next Step Today

Go pray some BOLD prayers.

What have you not been praying about because it seems impossible? One of the things God is best at is making the impossible turn into the possible. If the bold prayer request scares you a little, I promise you it won't intimidate God. He loves it when we come to Him with crazy faith!

One of my favorite things over the years has been to write down audaciously bold prayer requests in my journal and then look back at all the ones God brought to fruition.

Here's a list of a few of those requests:

- Marry Maddy.
- Raise $750,000 for our church to launch.
- See 1,000 people give their lives to Jesus in our first year as a church (we're currently at 300).
- For our friends to be able to have kids.
- For someone to donate a building for our church.

When God answers your daring-faith prayers, this gives you even more faith to go back to Him and ask for more! It's a beautiful cycle of faith and God's faithfulness. Today you should get bold with God!

Habit to Work Toward

Start a prayer journal and write down two different types of prayers:

1. Daily prayers—your prayers for that specific day. Whatever the Lord is speaking to you about, or whatever you may need specifically for that day.
2. Bold prayers—your prayers that would truly require a miracle from the Lord.

Truth to Believe

My big, bold prayer requests don't intimidate God; they delight Him.

19_

a critical spirit

The Problem

Having a critical spirit has become popular, accepted, and has even been encouraged.

By having a critical spirit, I mean being overly negative, constantly looking for the flaws in something or someone, and feeling the freedom to share those critical comments with others without restraint.

It seems the biggest YouTube channels, podcasts, and online influencers are building their platforms based on what they're against rather than what they're for.

The problem is that being critical of others is not a fruit of the Spirit or something followers of Jesus should find themselves engaged in.

The Solution

Instead of building through dishonor, build through honor. Instead of being overly critical, be overly faith-filled and life-giving. Be careful not to build your life, business, or ministry from being critical, negative, or dishonoring of others.

Romans 12:10 says, "Love one another with brotherly affection. Outdo one another in showing honor" (ESV). That word *outdo* means to compete! Paul is saying we should make it a competition to see who can be the most honoring toward others. That's how you look more like Christ—not through constant criticism or tearing down one another.

Here's the truth: you can build something fast by highlighting the negatives, but you can build things that *last* by highlighting the solutions. You can gain attention by talking about the way others have fallen short, but you can have real impact by casting a vision of how others have what it takes to do what needs to be done.

It's true that through dishonor you can gain quick attention. But if you build with dishonor, don't be surprised when what you build eventually dishonors you. Instead, take the high road and the more effective one. Build up! Don't tear down.

There's a simple yet powerful tweak to the way we talk about things that can help us have a spirit of honor: refuse to speak poorly of others. Just refuse! I've noticed that sometimes when I'm trying to honor someone or something really well, I might be tempted to compare it to other things or people who aren't as good. Yet this is just another form of dishonor. Other things don't have to be bad for you to talk about something or someone who is good!

As Christians we should be looking for the things in people that deserve recognition and calling these out. Jesus does this with us, and now we get to do it with others.

Next Step Today

Who is someone you could honor today?

We often think nice thoughts about people, but we fail to share them out loud. Think about someone who has made an impact on your life recently. It could be something big, or it could be something small. Have you honored them for that? If not, stop reading and do it right now!

a critical spirit

Recently I had someone in our church call me late at night. I was nervous to answer the phone because a call at that time of night normally doesn't mean something good. When I answered, I was so glad that I did.

It was one of our church volunteers calling to show thirty seconds of honor. He said, "I know it's late, and I'm so sorry. I just had a thought about something I've noticed in you and your wife. I've thought about it too many times without telling you, and I wanted that to change." He proceeded to speak life over us for thirty seconds and then said good night.

While the entire phone call lasted only two minutes or so, the encouragement to my soul lasted for weeks!

Your words are either tearing others down or building them up. Let's build today!

Habit to Work Toward

It can be hard to honor others every time we think good thoughts—after all, like me, you probably have lots of amazing people in your life.

Even so, I want to work toward the habit of honoring others as soon as I have the thought!

Imagine how much better our world would be with that kind of constant encouragement. I'm not there yet, but I'm trying. Let's work toward speaking life, and speaking it quickly and often.

Truth to Believe

My words have the power of life and death in them, so I will use mine to build others up.

20_
financial stewardship

The Problem

We often trade what we want most for what we want now.

This can be especially true with our money. Our paychecks hit our bank account, and we spend the money on what we want now. I want chipotle with double meat and guac now! I want a new car now! I want a bigger TV for watching college football now!

The problem with following these urges to spend now is that a few years down the road, we won't have what we want most and we will regret it.

We won't be debt-free like we want. We won't be able to live generously like we want. We won't have a home for our family like we want. We won't have financial stability like we want.

Instead of controlling our money, our money will be controlling us.

The Solution

Think long-term. Some of the most generous, joy-filled people I know have never made lots of money. They simply stewarded their money well, month after month and year after year. They began with a solid plan, and they stuck to it. This allowed them to do things financially that many of their peers—who likely make more money—had to miss out on.

financial stewardship

I like to think of dollars as little soldiers I send on missions. Every month I get a new batch of recruits. Many of them are in the infantry. They have the straightforward yet important role of paying the bills—the mortgage, utilities, electricity, groceries, etc. Other dollars are more like the Special Forces. I send them to our church in the form of tithe money to help further the gospel in Nashville. I send them to Cracker Barrel to help out the elderly man next to us, who's eating pancakes by himself. I send them to our investment account so they can set up base and recruit more soldiers to our cause.

The point is this: come up with a plan for your money. Without a plan to meet your long-term goals, it's hard to succeed. Our long-term goals are to tithe every month, give generously to others, get completely out of debt, and buy a house with an extra bedroom for our growing family. To accomplish these goals, this is what our monthly plan looks like:

- Tithe 10 percent of our income to our church on the first day of the month.
- Invest 10 percent of our income into more aggressive savings.
- Avoid using credit cards that accrue interest on debt.
- Budget $200 for giving to others as the Holy Spirit directs us.
- Automate as many of our bills as possible.

Each month we stay on top of these goals because we want to make sure we don't miss out on what we want most—for what we want now!

Next Step Today

Write down your goals.

What do you want your "soldier dollars" to accomplish? Do they have a mission? If not, then that is your first step today.

Remember to be specific. Don't make the mission something vague such as "I want to do better with my money." Your goals need to be specific so that they can be measured. If you can't measure them, they're probably not specific enough. Instead, make the mission something like "I want to save 10 percent of my total income this month," or "I want to stick to a budget of $300 for eating out this month."

When you set clear goals for yourself, you'll then be able to look back and check your progress. If you miss the mark one month, it's not the end of the world. But having those goals in place will help you correct course, so that a month doesn't turn into three months of missing the mark.

You don't have to be perfect, but the main objective should be to become a better steward of your money. Your future self and family will thank you for it!

Habit to Work Toward

A habit that has been a fun game changer for my wife and me is to have a monthly business meeting.

We keep it simple. Basically we sit down and go through our bank statement, then assess what money we spent and where we spent it. We look at everything by category: giving, investing, bills, eating out, groceries, diapers and wipes (lol), and entertainment (fun money).

This is one of the most helpful things we do in monitoring our finances and something we look back on to check our progress. Again, if you aren't regularly measuring your goals, it's going to be hard to hit them!

Truth to Believe

God has called me to be a good steward of everything He's put in my hands, including my money.

21_

tithing

The Problem

Money is an idol many people don't know they have.

This is one of the reasons Jesus talked so much about money. Out of His 39 parables, 16 of them were about money. There are roughly 500 verses in the Bible about faith, 500 about prayer, and 500 about obedience. There are over 2,000 verses about money.

Why? It's not because God wants the money in our pockets or bank accounts; it's because He wants this idol out of our hearts.

The Solution

When my wife and I had our first child, we were so excited to hear what his first spoken words would be. Just as I so victoriously predicted, our son Lion's first word was "Dada."

But his second word? "Mine."

From a very young age, we feel a tug to gain and protect what's "mine." As we get older, however, the *mine* we want to protect is no longer things like toys or graham crackers. No, it's usually money.

In Matthew 6:21, Jesus says, "For where your treasure is, there your heart will be also." A short statement that is *full* of wisdom and conviction. Jesus could see straight into the hearts of people and understood that, for most of us, the thing we often think about, worry over, and try to protect is our money.

But God doesn't want us to lead lives where we're always thinking about money. He wants us to live in a way where we're always thinking about *Him*. So how do we do that? How do we stop thinking about money all the time—money that pays our bills, allows us to eat, maintain a roof over our heads, not to mention have a little fun?

Enter the concept of tithing.

Tithing is simply the act of giving the Lord 10 percent of your income. I know what you're thinking. *Wait, Noah, I thought you said you were going to help me worry less about money, and now you're telling me to give 10 percent of my income to God?*

Exactly.

Tithing has been the single greatest gift to my relationship with my finances. The first reason I tithe is because I believe the Bible instructs us to. When I first started to tithe, that was the *only* reason I did it. But as I've continued the practice, it's transformed my life! Every month when I give 10 percent back to God, it's a tangible reminder to my soul that it is God who sits on the throne of my life, not my money. It reminds me that God is my provider and not me, my job, or my boss.

To top it all off, tithing has opened the doorway to generosity in my life. It's shown me a way for my money to be used based on a mission, to help build God's kingdom—my money, my time, and my talents.

Tithing has helped me to see I was born selfish, but I was born again generous.

Next Step Today

Maybe tithing 10 percent seems like too big of a next step for you. If so, let's try generosity in baby steps.

What if today you made the choice to be generous in some way to somebody that you didn't have to? Maybe that means paying for the person behind you at the coffee shop or restaurant. Maybe it means sending a coworker a gift card or some money, just because.

One thing I've noticed about generosity is that it's contagious. Once you start, you can't stop. And soon other people want to join in on the fun.

Jesus said it is better to give than to receive (see Acts 20:35). I wasn't so sure about that for a long time. But now? Now I couldn't agree more with this profound truth.

It's a blessing to give to others. And doing so makes us more like Jesus.

Habit to Work Toward

Try tithing.

My wife and I, on the first of every month, give 10 percent of our month's paycheck to our local church. At first it was hard. Now it's a delight. In fact, we often give more than 10 percent because of how much fun it is to live a life of generosity.

Do it with an open mind and an open heart. Your soul will be blessed in ways you may be surprised by.

Truth to Believe

I get to be generous to others because God has been so generous to me.

22_

accountability

The Problem

We don't like it when people tell us hard things. More specifically, we don't like accountability.

We live in a culture that encourages us to keep only those people in our lives who agree with us and support us, who never offend us in any way. Our culture says if someone says something to you that doesn't completely support you and what you're doing, you should cut them out of your life.

The problem is that this advice leads to your circle of friends being a group of yes-men. It leads to your missing out on truth and wisdom. More importantly, it leads to missing out on becoming more like Jesus.

The Solution

Imagine that you have a toxic habit, something really bad. Although it's killing you, you can't see it.

Your friends say nothing to you about your habit because they don't want to offend you. They believe the conversation would be awkward and that you would probably get upset, so they don't want to risk saying anything. They'd rather that you

accountability

harm yourself than you be upset with them. They're thinking of themselves and not you.

But there's one friend who disagrees with the others about staying quiet. He clearly sees how your toxic habit is ruining your life. So he decides to speak up and tell you what you need to hear even though it's not easy. Ignoring his own feelings and whether you might get upset with him, he forges ahead, knowing you'll be better off in the long run if you are told the truth about your habit and how it's taking you down. He's not thinking about himself; he's thinking only of you.

Sometimes the hardest things to hear are spoken out of the deepest places of love. You need more friends like this one friend.

In John 8:32, Jesus said, "You will know the truth, and the truth will set you free." We need friends who will tell us the whole truth. Truth is often uncomfortable, but if you don't have people in your life who have been given permission to be honest with you, holding nothing back, you may be living in captivity and not even know it.

Imagine if the disciples had not been willing to receive uncomfortable truth from Jesus. They would have missed out on a lot. Imagine what we might miss out on if we cut out of our lives every person who cares enough about us to call us out when we're heading down a dangerous path.

Among the greatest blessings in my life are those close friends who are willing to tell me the truth to my face, even though it's hard and uncomfortable. They're not afraid to talk to me, to help me see what I can't see myself! Have there been times when one of them said something to me that I didn't receive well? Absolutely. Yet almost every time I've come around to the fact that they were in the right. I just had too much pride to believe them at first.

Do you have any friends who love you enough to tell you the truth? Don't shun these friends, but keep them close.

Next Step Today

Not long ago a young man at our church asked me to meet him for coffee. Once seated at the coffee shop, he blurted out, "Noah, I want to give you permission to hold me accountable."

He went on to share how he'd been drifting in his relationship with the Lord, which had consequences in other areas of his life as well. He wanted to meet with me to ask if I would hold him accountable concerning things like his participating at church, his attitude, and giving. But before he requested that I hold him accountable, he first gave me permission to do so.

Have you given your friends permission to hold you accountable, or are you just hoping they will?

You may have people in your life who want to hold you accountable, and who would like you to do the same for them, but they're waiting for your permission. Your next step is to give it to them.

Habit to Work Toward

This habit is one I'm particularly excited to share with you because it's yielded so much fruit in my life.

I encourage you to work toward the habit of texting your close circle of friends once per month and asking them to tell you how you're doing. I send this text out on the first of every month. My most recent text went something like this:

> Hey, guys, I'd love your honest thoughts—how am I doing? Is there any area in my life that seems unhealthy or out of sync to you? (Besides how many donuts I ate at Connor's house!) Thanks for helping me become the man God wants me to be.

Sometimes the responses are all positive. Other times there are real moments of accountability. And I thank God for those because, little by little, I'm becoming more like Christ.

Truth to Believe

Friends who love me enough to tell me the truth are the best kind of friends.

23_

the church

The Problem

It's become almost cool to look down on the Church, some even going so far as to hate the Church. The problem is that Jesus *loves* the Church.

Jesus himself started the Church. The disciples died while building the Church. Jesus is for the Church. Jesus called the Church His bride. As Christians we ought to love the Church too.

We can't say we love Jesus while simultaneously looking down on His Church.

The Solution

The solution is to build God's Church.

Do we ignore all the harm the Church has caused people? Do we ignore all the instances of various churches operating poorly, of pastors behaving badly or even illegally? Of course not. These abuses break our hearts. Countless people have dealt with hurtful experiences at their local church that they can point to. I've learned, though, it's unhelpful and unwise to judge the majority who are trying to do things right by the minority who got it wrong.

I've seen the bad side of the Church, but I've also seen the good side!

I've seen a teenager pray with other teenagers, and their family accept Christ because of it. I've seen a $200,000 hospital bill be paid by an anonymous person in the Church. I've seen healing and restoration in the Church. I've seen a man in his mid-seventies be set free from an addiction of sixty-plus years in the Church. I've seen isolated, lonely people find family in the Church. I've seen people exchange their drugs for a Bible in the Church. I've seen people go from being haters to builders in the Church! I've seen what can happen through the Church!

The Church has outlasted empires, kingdoms, and cultures. The Church will never die or become irrelevant because Jesus lives and reigns supreme, and always will. The Church is alive!

So find a church community, join the team, and start building. Don't fall for the lie of the enemy that says you don't need church. Consider this quote by Tony Evans:

> You don't need church to be a Christian. You also don't need to go home to be married. But stay away long enough and the relationship will be affected.

When I'm committed to a local church, I'm around the body of Christ, where I can be sharpened and challenged by other believers. I can be encouraged and uplifted. I can more effectively live out the calling of God on my life. More importantly, I can be a part of the community Jesus was so excited to see thrive.

I don't want to spend my life building my dream. I want to build His dream, and His dream is the Church.

Next Step Today

If you aren't a part of a local church, your next step is to find one.

Something to keep in mind as you look: there are no perfect churches. Here are a few questions to ask yourself when you step into a church:

1. Do they teach the Bible, or do they teach something else?
2. Do they have a community you'd be excited to be a part of?
3. Do they serve with a sense of mission in your town or city and seek to help others?

If they do these three things, you're on the right path! There are a ton of personal preferences that people have when it comes to church, but these three are essential and should be nonnegotiable. If you find such a church, your next step is not to put one foot in and one foot out. Go all in! Don't just be a spectator at church; be a builder.

Habit to Work Toward

Go to church regularly.

According to research done by the Barna Group, the average churchgoer attends services about once every five weeks. To be blunt, that's not enough.

Church attendance doesn't get us into heaven, but being a part of a life-giving church helps get heaven into us! We should make church a priority in our lives by consistently showing up—helping to build the Church, serving and being a blessing to others for Jesus' sake.

Truth to Believe

Because Jesus loves the Church, it's an honor for me to serve the Church.

24_

the more-monster

The Problem

The more-monster is on the loose, and he's taking victims captive.

What exactly is the more-monster? It's that little voice inside your head that tells you if you could just have *more* ____, then you'd be happy. More money. More followers. More success. More affirmation. More approval. More property, a bigger house.

The problem is that the more-monster is a liar. Time after time we get what we've been chasing after, and we hope to finally silence that little voice in our heads, only to find the voice growing louder.

The problem is that *more* doesn't satisfy the human soul. Instead, it works to frustrate the soul.

The Solution

Contentment kills the more-monster, and yet finding contentment is way easier said than done.

I once had a conversation with an older man who exuded contentment. He didn't come across as someone who is striving or trying to earn the approval of others and yet he's very successful at what he does. I told him that one of the things I admired most about him was his genuine contentment and asked him if he had any tips for someone like me who loves setting goals and chasing them. His response surprised me:

"Goals are good, Noah. Set them. God is better. Sit with Him. Your number one goal should be that your goals never become your gods. A desire for excellence is not wrong. A desire for excellence over a desire for God is wrong. The only way I've been able to balance it the right way is by sitting with God each morning and reminding myself that He is my prize."

If you want to live a contented life, you must live in the reality that God is your prize. The apostle Paul was a great example of this. Just look at what he says in Philippians 4:12–13:

> I have learned the secret of being content in any and every situation, whether well fed or hungry, whether living in plenty or in want. I can do all this through him who gives me strength.

Paul realized that true contentment doesn't come from getting more stuff. True contentment comes from getting more of God. The more we get of Him, the more we can see the lies of the more-monster from far away. The more we get of God, the more our souls come to the realization that nothing on this earth will ever truly satisfy us.

You don't "make it" when you reach all your goals or get all the stuff you want. You "make it" when Jesus is enough for you.

Next Step Today

I don't know if it's because I struggle a bit with materialism or if it's just a good thing for people to do, but one of the most practical things that helps me stay content is to regularly get rid of STUFF.

By *stuff* I mean everything: clothes, toys, books, worn furniture, tools—everything! My rule is simple: if I haven't thought about the thing or used it in a year, then I need to sell it, give it away, or throw it in the trash. Stuff can be addictive. By regularly purging my life of excess, this helps me keep the main thing the main thing in my life. And it helps keep the house tidy.

Your next step today is to do a deep cleaning of your house or apartment. What have you been keeping around that needs to go? Be hard on yourself and get rid of as much as possible. We need things a lot less than we think we do, and once they're gone, it frees us up to focus on the things we do need. The primary thing being a person: God.

Habit to Work Toward

Before you buy something that costs more than $100, unless it's a necessity, wait for two weeks.

This is a great habit to form to fight the more-monster. Two weeks allows enough time to make sure we actually want and need the thing we are considering purchasing instead of making an impulse decision based on emotion.

It helps us make purchases out of a place of contentment instead of out of a place of greed, of always wanting *more*.

Truth to Believe

There is only one "more" that will truly satisfy me, and that is in having more of Christ.

25_
anxiety

The Problem

Anxiety is an ongoing problem that distresses many people on a daily basis.

There are so many things we can worry about these days: work, school, family, relationships, the stock market, things we see on the news, things we read on social media. We worry about things that may not even be happening yet, but because we're on a worry roll, we continue to worry about them anyway!

Anxiety/worry is like a rocking chair: it gives you something to do, but gets you nowhere. In fact, it gets you worse than nowhere. The problem with worry is that it causes you to put your faith in the wrong outcome.

The Solution

The solution to worry is prayer.

Philippians 4:6–7 says, "Do not be anxious about anything, but in every situation, by prayer and petition, with thanksgiving, present your requests to God. And the peace of God, which transcends all understanding, will guard your hearts and your minds in Christ Jesus."

The disciples had front-row seats to the life and ministry of Jesus. They saw Him preach to thousands of people. They saw Him feed those thousands with just five loaves of bread and two fish. They saw Him heal the afflicted, calm a raging storm, even raise the dead back to life. And yet in the book of Luke, chapter 11, the disciples don't ask Jesus to teach them how to do any of those things. Instead, they ask Him to teach them how to pray.

Why? I believe it's because they had witnessed all the miraculous things Jesus had done, and they were convinced they'd started with prayer.

Prayer is *powerful*. In my life I've known prayer to change three things: prayer changes situations; prayer changes other people; and prayer changes me. When we pray, we're inviting God into what's going on. And wherever God is invited, things change.

While worry changes nothing, prayer changes everything.

When I find myself worrying about something, whether it's big or small, what I'm really having a hard time doing is trusting God. Think about it. We worry about finances because we aren't trusting God as our provider. We worry about relationships because we don't trust God to work things out for us. We worry about plans because we don't really trust God to do what's best for us.

Worry, then, is a trust problem. Where you're worrying the most shows where you're trusting God the least.

One of the greatest benefits of prayer is that it helps us learn to trust God. When we turn our eyes away from what's causing us to worry and direct them on our Savior, we're reminded that He has our best interests in mind, and there's no situation that scares or alarms Him.

Are you worried today?

Jesus said,

"Come to me, all you who are weary and burdened, and I will give you rest. Take my yoke upon you and learn from me, for I am gentle and humble in heart, and you will find rest for your souls. For my yoke is easy and my burden is light."

Matthew 11:28–30

Talk to Jesus. Trust Him. He cares.

Next Step Today

Try the one-minute prayer.

For a lot of people, the idea of talking to God through prayer can be intimidating at first. We don't know what to say, and we often don't have a lot to say. It can feel weird!

The great news is that God wants us to talk with Him like we do with one of our friends—and it's not nearly as hard as you might think.

Something I love to do is to take breaks throughout my day just to talk to God for sixty seconds at a time. No matter where you are on your prayer journey, I guarantee you that you can pray for one minute! I've found that the more often I take that one minute to talk to God, the less my worry and anxiety tend to talk to me.

Imagine how different you might feel today if you stopped a couple of times for sixty seconds to include God in your decisions, in your plans, and in your work? It could literally change everything for you. Instead of worrying, you'd be praying!

Got a promotion at work today? Celebrate with God for one minute.

Have a big decision to make in a relationship? Ask God for wisdom for one minute.

anxiety

Running out of gas on the interstate? Pray for an exit, quick! I heard a preacher once say, "God goes where He's wanted." I believe that to be true. I also believe that God speaks to those who want to speak to Him.

Habit to Work Toward

Try the one-minute prayer throughout your day.

I do the one-minute prayer after every single thing on my calendar now. Here's how this looked today, a random Tuesday:

5:30 a.m. – quiet time

6:00 a.m. – go for a run

7:00 a.m. – shower and breakfast

8:00 a.m. – wake kids up and feed them

9:00 a.m. – start writing sermon for church on Sunday

12:00 p.m. – lunch with friend

1:00 p.m. – staff meeting

3:00 p.m. – coffee with church member

4:30 p.m. – go home to see the kids

5:00 p.m. – start cooking dinner

6:00 p.m. – dinner

6:30 p.m. – play with kids

7:30 p.m. – put kids down to sleep

8:00 p.m. – hang out with my wife

That's fourteen different things I did today, and after each one of them I talked to God for sixty seconds. Which means today I talked to God for fourteen minutes. It would have been way more difficult for me to sit quietly in a room and talk to God for fourteen minutes straight at one time. But the one-minute prayer throughout the day allows me to talk to God in a way that feels natural. It's an ongoing conversation. I believe God wants that from us—and we should want this as well.

Truth to Believe

Prayer has the power to change everything in my life.

26_

cycle of sin

The Problem

It can be hard to stop sinning when you've been sinning in some area repeatedly for a long time. Not just hard, but brutally hard.

I battled a certain cycle of sin in my life for years, and no matter how hard I tried, and no matter how badly I wanted to, I just couldn't shake it. I would win a few battles here and there, but overwhelmingly it felt as though I was losing the war.

The problem is that, although our spirit is willing, our flesh is weak.

The Solution

Let's start with what the solution to your cycle of sin is not:

The solution is not in applying more willpower. It's probably not greater knowledge about why what you're doing is wrong. Accountability will definitely help you, but that too isn't going to be enough to win the war here. What you need is something much stronger.

I wrestled with an addiction to pornography for years. I didn't find freedom from this when I began going to church. I didn't find freedom when I joined a small group. I didn't find freedom when I started reading my Bible. All of those things are important and vital for Christian people, and I'd encourage you to do them if you're not already doing so, but they didn't lead to my freedom from the cycle of sin.

I was set free when I found Jesus more beautiful than my sin. That's it. That's the whole secret. You see, when Jesus is more beautiful than the sin you keep running back to, you won't run to it anymore. Instead, you'll run to *Him*!

We get it all backward. We think if we just try harder, strategize more effectively, or find the right mix of accountability, we won't do that *thing* anymore—whatever it is you find yourself enslaved to. But it's not true! We don't overcome our sin by fighting harder; we overcome our sin by falling in love.

So how does that happen? Work backward with me. If you want to find Jesus more beautiful than your sin, then you need to fall in love with Him.

If you want to fall in love with Him, then you need to spend time with Him. To spend time with Him, you need to sit with Him. Ending the cycle of sin in your life begins with sitting with Jesus.

There are a lot of different ways to "sit with Jesus." You could pray. You could read your Bible. You could simply sit in silence in His presence, your thoughts focused on Him. You could worship Him through music. Or you could go on a walk and talk to Him while being surrounded by nature. The point is not *how* you sit with Him—it's that you do it often.

This takes time. You've got all sorts of junk that has piled up in the corners of your heart. And the best way to get rid of all the junk is to let Him in.

Next Step Today

If you're desperate to quit the cycle of sin in your life, today is the day to pray a simple prayer of submission. I've written one out for you:

> *Lord Jesus, I give up trying to beat this sin on my own. First, I ask you to forgive me. I know you will, and I'm so grateful for that. But now I ask that you strengthen me.*
>
> *Give me the strength to recognize that what I've been trying to do is not working. I want to live a holy life like you've called me to, and I realize the most effective way to do that is not by getting all the bad stuff out, but by getting more of you in! That's what I want, God—more of you and less of me.*
>
> *Today I make the intentional decision to pursue you. I know you've been pursuing me, but I want to pursue you now. I want to sit with you and learn from you. I want to get to know you better and ultimately fall more in love with you than with the feelings I get from my sin.*
>
> *Jesus, I need you. Amen.*

Habit to Work Toward

Sit with Jesus every day.

Don't just try to do it; make a plan to do it. If you let your day happen and you don't plan out when you're going to sit with Jesus, you will look up at the end of the day and realize it didn't happen.

Prioritize. If Jesus is as important in your life as you say He is, then you'll make time to sit with Him every day.

Truth to Believe

Jesus is far more beautiful than my sin.

27_

opinions

The Problem

We care too much about what people think of us.

The thing that keeps people from obeying God more than anything else is the opinions of others. There are two problems with this: (a) God's opinion should matter more; and (b) very few people are actually thinking about you.

According to a recent study by Harvard, it's estimated that people think or talk about us just 3 percent of the amount of time we believe they do.

What a tragedy it is that we let people who didn't die for us affect how we obey the One who did.

The Solution

I've had the honor of sitting down with a man who has lived a long and full life. He'd grown quite old and knew he had only a short time left on this earth. I was so grateful to spend a little time with him; he talked about his life and shared stories with me that not only made me laugh but taught me something.

Toward the end of our conversation, I leaned in and asked him one final question. "If you could start your life over," I said, "what's one thing you would do differently?"

opinions

His answer: "I'd stop caring so much about what people thought about me."

Aristotle said it this way: "To avoid criticism: say nothing, do nothing, and be nothing."

To be faithful, say everything, do everything, and be everything God has asked you to be no matter what other people say or think.

Noah, in the book of Genesis, looked like a fool until it started to rain. Moses looked to be out of his mind until the Red Sea split into two. The disciples too looked as if out of their minds—that is, until Jesus rose from the dead!

One thing is for sure: if you decide to follow Jesus with everything you have, people aren't going to understand some of your decisions. But something else is for sure: you will never regret radical obedience to Jesus.

The truth is that we *should* care about the opinion of someone. That opinion is the opinion of Jesus. Am I obeying Him? Am I doing His will? Am I following His ways? When we do this, everything works out the way it should in our lives. Put God first and He will do the heavy lifting in your life.

I like to think about it like this: obedience is my job; the outcome is God's.

Next Step Today

Identify whose opinions hold too much weight in your life.

Now, what I'm *not* saying here is to live your life without ever taking people's opinions into consideration. That would be foolish. In fact, the book of Proverbs encourages us to seek the wise counsel of others. So I'm not telling you to stop listening to people. What I am saying is that we need to listen to the *right* people.

For example, you shouldn't give too much weight to someone's opinion about your dating relationship who has never been in a dating relationship. But you should deeply care about the opinion coming from someone who has been in a healthy marriage for a long time.

You shouldn't give too much weight to someone's opinion about your finances if they're broke. But you should listen intently to someone who handles their money well and has a proven track record of good stewardship.

You shouldn't give too much weight to someone's opinion about your spiritual life if they don't believe in Jesus. But if your pastor is trying to give you advice on how to follow Jesus, you should probably listen.

Take a step back today and assess the opinions of others you're listening to. Is there anyone you're listening to that you shouldn't be? Does their opinion run counter to what Jesus is asking of you?

Habit to Work Toward

The negative feedback of others is never easy to receive. That's why a good habit to work toward is not to make any decisions immediately after you've received negative or harsh feedback.

Receive it. Stay calm and let it simmer for a day. Go to bed. Then wake up the next morning and pray about it. Is there any truth in what they said to you? Or is it just an opinion that you shouldn't heed or listen to?

Truth to Believe

Other people's opinions should never keep me from obeying God.

28

finding a good wife

The Problem

Finding a good wife is *hard*. For a man, outside of your decision to follow Jesus, there's no other decision as important as who you will marry. This decision will affect your future family, your career, and your calling. This decision needs to be made very wisely.

The Solution

You need to know what to look for.

So many guys looking to find a good wife are struggling because they're looking at all the wrong things. Of course you want an attractive wife, but is her soul as attractive as her profile picture? Yeah, it's really cool to be with a girl who is consistently the popular girl, but is she consistently spending time with God? It might not mean a lot to you right now that she doesn't seem to have many friends who are girls, but is there a reason for that?

What you need to do is to approach looking for a wife with what my mom used to call "long-term eyes."

Short-term eyes look at things that don't age well. Long-term eyes look at things that will go the distance. Short-term eyes might be good for a first date. Long-term eyes are good for a wedding ring.

To put it plainly: you don't want to marry a girl; you want to marry a woman of God. You don't want to look for Ms. Right Now; you want to look for Ms. Right Forever.

A woman of God won't ask you to be a man of compromise. A woman of God won't lead you on intentionally. A woman of God will use her words to build you up, not tear you down. A woman of God won't find her identity in being in a relationship with you. A woman of God will pray for you without you asking her.

A woman of God will pursue Jesus more than she pursues you.

Next Step Today

One of the best ways to get long-term eyes is to go to the Bible and read what it says about a godly woman. And the best place for that can be found in Proverbs, chapter 31.

This chapter defines what has become known as the "Proverbs 31 woman." It describes a woman of noble character. A woman who will make a great wife.

When I was single, I would often read Proverbs 31 and then pray for my future wife. This helped remind me of what I was looking for in a wife. And when she finally did walk into my life, I didn't hesitate to approach her. After all, I had been praying for her!

Try it for yourself! Read Proverbs 31 and see if this chapter helps you as you search for "a wife of noble character." Who knows? There may be someone you've been overlooking—you just need new eyes.

Habit to Work Toward

Pray for your future spouse.

God hears your prayers, so why would you not pray about a decision as important as finding/choosing your spouse? A great habit to work toward is to pray for a few moments each day that God would make the right woman obvious to you, and the wrong women just as obvious.

Lord Jesus, give me eyes only for the one you have for me. Amen.

Truth to Believe

Having a godly perspective will help me find a godly wife.

29_

singleness

The Problem

Many of us view singleness as a negative, as a kind of sickness. The problem is that singleness is *not* a sickness, and relationships are not the cure.

If you aren't happy or content being single, entering a relationship will only be a Band-Aid covering a deeper problem. Relationships are meant to sharpen us, not satisfy us. Only Jesus can satisfy us fully.

The Solution

Make the most of your singleness by viewing singleness for what it is: a blessing.

Here are four perspective-changers on singleness:

1. Singleness offers you the chance to make Jesus your foundation.
   Use this season to make sure God is truly your prize and not a relationship status. It's an unbelievable joy to know that if/when you do step into a relationship one day, you've built your life on the right foundation already.

singleness

2. Singleness offers you time.
When you're single, you have more time to do what you want than you ever will again. More time to serve the Lord, build a business, explore your interests and hobbies, and hang out with friends. Once a relationship, marriage, and a family come along, your free time gets smaller and smaller with each new addition. Of course, these phases of life bring lots of blessing to your life as well. Still, one of the huge blessings of the season of singleness is that you have *time*. Make the most of it!

3. Singleness means you can establish healthy rhythms.
There's no better time to establish good, healthy habits than when you're single: exercise, Bible reading/study, investing money, and learning new things. Again, because you have extra time, you can direct your life in a healthy direction.

4. Singleness offers you the opportunity for strong friendships.
There's no better time to invest in strong friendships than when you're single. Say yes to a spontaneous trip. Meet weekly for coffee. Go on adventures and make memories with your friends. When you start dating or get married, the truth is that you'll need to dedicate a lot of your time to your relationship/spouse. That doesn't mean you won't still enjoy great friendships; you just won't have the same amount of time to spend with these people. So invest heavily now!

These are just a few of the massive pros that come with singleness. If you are single but really want to get married, that's a good, perfectly natural desire. Just don't wish away your current season that's full of blessings.

It's possible to be excited about your future marriage while enjoying your current singleness.

Next Step Today

Create a singleness bucket list.

One of the things that attracted me to my wife, Maddy, was how she approached her singleness. She wasn't waiting around for some man to come along and fulfill her. She had a *full* life to live, and she was living it!

In fact, she'd created a list of things she wanted to do and experience while single to help her make the most of this season of her life. Her list included:

- Read through the Bible in a year.
- Go skydiving.
- Study abroad in Europe.
- Travel with her ten best friends to Colorado.
- Visit Paris during Fashion Week.
- Work out three times a week.

By making a list of things she wanted to do, she was reminding herself that the season of singleness could and should be a great one full of exciting new adventures and memories.

Your next step today is to create a list of your own. What could you do while single that would have you looking back one day in the future and saying, "I made the most of it"?

Habit to Work Toward

One of the most common things people say a few years after getting married and starting a family is, "I didn't realize how much time I wasted when single until I got married."

Don't let those words be something that comes out of your mouth in the future. Make the most of your time now! A great habit to start is the habit of using a planner. Plan your responsibilities, daily tasks, and meetings, but also use it to plan for fun, like enjoying hobbies and going on adventures. You'll want to make the most of the season of singleness, and planning to do so is a good first step.

Truth to Believe

Singleness is not a sickness at all. Singleness is a blessing.

30_

gratitude

The Problem

We take things for granted so easily, which leads to unhappiness and a lack of joy.

Because of things like comparison, distraction, and sin in our lives, we regularly overlook our blessings in search of something more. When we do this, the result can be a life of entitlement, jealousy, and pride.

The Solution

The secret to joy is gratitude, and as Christians, there should be no one more grateful than us.

Last year my wife, Maddy, threw me a surprise birthday party. It was the first time anyone has done something like that for me since I was a little kid. All my closest friends were there. There was cake and miniature golf and so many other little things that I started crying. I was so overwhelmed by the kindness shown to me.

My wife's birthday is coming up, and you better believe I'll be planning the best party ever for her. Why? Because when someone throws you a party, it makes you want to throw others a party.

gratitude

As men of God, we should be party-throwers filled with gratitude because of the party Jesus threw for us when we put our faith and trust in Him. We know we could never have deserved or earned the party Jesus gave us, which should make us even more grateful to Him!

Most people practice gratitude when they feel blessed. We already know that we're blessed and so we practice gratitude at all times. There's a big difference!

In Philippians 4:4, Paul says, "Rejoice in the Lord always. I will say it again: Rejoice!" We can be grateful every single day and no matter our circumstances because we have Jesus in our hearts and lives. In fact, if God didn't do another thing for me, I would already be the most blessed person of all time because of what Jesus did for me on the cross.

Yet our God is so good that He didn't just stop at the cross. He continues to pour out blessings on us every day. Now we get to choose to acknowledge them and practice gratitude!

Have you ever met a truly grateful person? Someone who is just exuding gratitude, not just for the big things but for the small things as well. Their attitude is contagious. When you spend time with someone like that, you immediately want to be friends with them.

That's the kind of life we're called to live. Not the selfish and entitled life the world says is normal. No, we are men filled with gratitude!

Next Step Today

It's been said that you could change the world with all the unexpressed gratitude inside people's heads. Meaning we don't express gratitude nearly as often as we should, and if we did, our world would be a much better place.

What if your next step today was simply to express gratitude to the people in your life? Maybe that means calling your boss and thanking him for always having your best interests in mind.

Maybe it means telling your parents that you're grateful for the way they raised you and provided for you when growing up.

Maybe it means telling the barista at the coffee shop that you're grateful for the way they treat you with kindness every time you buy a coffee from them.

Maybe it means telling Jesus how grateful you are for Him paying for your sins.

When we look for reasons to be grateful, we often find even more reasons to be grateful. Let's have an attitude of rejoicing always, expressing our gratitude to God and to others, thanking them for the many blessings in our lives.

Habit to Work Toward

Begin your prayer time each morning with gratitude and with worship, which is a great habit to work toward on a daily basis. Before you start talking to God about your needs and concerns, tell Him what it is you're grateful for.

Truth to Believe

Because of Jesus' love and sacrifice for me, I'm truly blessed. I have so much to be grateful for.

31_

the holy spirit

The Problem

People have been taught poorly about the Holy Spirit.

In fact, because of weird past experiences, many believers get uncomfortable when the Holy Spirit is brought up in conversation and tend to shy away from the Holy Spirit as much as possible.

This is a massive problem for many reasons, but the main one is that the Holy Spirit is just as much a part of the Trinity as God the Father and Jesus the Son.

We shouldn't be afraid of the Holy Spirit. We should be afraid of trying to do life without the Holy Spirit.

The Solution

We need a healthy and biblically accurate view of the Holy Spirit so that we can have a great relationship with the Spirit.

First, the Holy Spirit is not a thing or an "it." The Holy Spirit is a person. Second, the Holy Spirit is not weird—it's people who tend to be weird.

You may have seen some weird things in church or outside of church that were said to be the manifestation of the Holy

Spirit. We need to separate the weird from the supernatural. I have met lots of weird people. I've met lots of weird people *at church*. And that's a good thing! The Church and Jesus are for everyone! But just because a person says something is the Holy Spirit doesn't make it the Holy Spirit.

At the same time, the Holy Spirit is supernatural. All of Christianity is supernatural when you think about it. If you removed the supernatural from the Bible, you wouldn't have a book—you would have a sticky note. Jesus Christ being raised from the dead is pretty supernatural! We can expect a whole lot more supernatural stuff to come from the person of the Holy Spirit because He too is God.

So don't let so-called weird things keep you from the supernatural things the Holy Spirit wants to do in your life.

With the Holy Spirit we have a comforter. We have someone living inside of us who gives us the same power that raised Christ from the dead. With the Holy Spirit we have a guide who is always with us to help us become more like Jesus. The Holy Spirit helps us to discern, to have courage, and to speak the truth in love.

Without the Holy Spirit we are weak, worldly, and ultimately can do very little right. But with the Holy Spirit we are more than conquerors, we can live holy lives, and we can do things only God can get the credit for.

Don't run from the Holy Spirit. Run to the Holy Spirit.

Next Step Today

Meet with the Holy Spirit.

I once had a dream about Michael Jordan. In the dream, he and I were drinking cappuccinos at a coffee shop and talking about basketball. Amazing, right?

Then suddenly he took off his mask, and I was no longer sitting with Michael Jordan in this dream. I was sitting with my friend Jake! Then I woke up.

Now imagine it's the next day. I get a call from a number I don't recognize, and it's the real Michael Jordan! He asks me if I will meet with him for coffee. But instead of jumping at the opportunity of a lifetime, I let my past bad experience with the fake Michael Jordan keep me from a life-changing experience with the real one.

That would be ridiculous!

Don't let a past misrepresentation of the Holy Spirit keep you from opening your heart to the Spirit and His working in your life. Stop and pray this simple prayer:

Holy Spirit, I love you. I want to meet with you today. I invite you to come be with me, to guide me in my life. Make me aware of what you're saying to me and leading me to do. Amen.

Habit to Work Toward

A mentor told me he prays to the Holy Spirit before he meets with friends and colleagues: "Holy Spirit, what do you see in the person I'm about to meet with that I could say out loud?"

In other words, he wishes to voice out loud what God sees in his friends, to bless and encourage them. What a powerful concept. What if we developed this habit of listening to the Holy Spirit and then speaking life over our friends?

Truth to Believe

The Holy Spirit is God, and He wants to meet with and speak to me every day.

32_
pride vs. humility

The Problem

As Jesus followers, pride is one of the deadliest things we can have in our lives. It's also one of the hardest to detect. The prideful person is often the last one to know they have pride, though everyone else can see it.

The Bible tells us, "Pride goes before destruction, a haughty spirit before a fall" (Proverbs 16:18). Later on, the Bible says, "God opposes the proud but shows favor to the humble" (1 Peter 5:5).

The problem is that pride is a sneaky, quiet destroyer of our souls and our relationships with God.

The Solution

The solution to pride is leading a life of humility.

In the same Scripture where we learn that God opposes the proud, we learn that God gives grace to the humble. The word *grace* means unmerited favor and love. This is huge! The Bible tells us that we're given the *favor* of God when we lead lives of humility instead of pride. But what *is* humility?

Humility is not thinking less of ourselves; it's thinking of ourselves less.

Humility is not having low self-esteem; it's having low self-absorption and self-importance.

Pride always has its eyes fixed on *me*. What's in it for *me*? What will people think about *me*? But humility fixes its eyes on others. What's in this for others? How can I help or serve others?

Pride walks into a room and says, "Here I am." But humility walks into the room with the attitude and spirit of, "There you are!"

Humility is something that doesn't come natural to most men. It's hard to live a truly humble life. But we're blessed in that we have Jesus to turn to as the supreme example of what true humility looks like. Philippians 2:8 says, "And being found in appearance as a man, he [Jesus] humbled himself by becoming obedient to death—even death on a cross!"

Jesus is God and yet He humbled himself, left His Father's side in heaven, and became flesh and blood, a human being among us. His earthly ministry culminated as He sacrificed himself on the cross for our sins. That is love, and that is the ultimate humility!

Jesus' humility changes lives every day. Your humility can also change lives.

Imagine the impact you could have by being a man who pursues excellence in all you do, but who makes success about others instead of about yourself.

Imagine being a boss who gives the credit for a strong quarter to your coworkers instead of taking the credit yourself.

Imagine being an athlete who scores the winning goal, but who wants to talk about his teammates' contributions rather than himself.

Imagine being a man God uses mightily who gives all the glory to God, not accepting any glory for yourself.

That's who you can be. That's who you *are*. A humble servant of the Lord who has the favor of God on his life.

Next Step Today

One practical way we can develop a heart that's humble is by serving people who can give us nothing in return. We are called to serve others, and we're never more like Jesus than when we serve those who have no way of paying us back.

Is there someone you can serve today who is disadvantaged in any way? Maybe you have a car and this person doesn't, so you can offer them a ride to where they need to go. Maybe there's a person experiencing homelessness you see every day at the street corner, and you could offer them a meal or a gift card. Maybe there's someone who works for you who you can publicly honor and show kindness to when they least expect it.

Humility may not be easy, but it's possible—through one act after another of humbling yourself and by serving others.

Habit to Work Toward

"I'm not the star on this team."

We need to hear this quote regularly and take it to heart. Because of our human nature, we often buy into the lie that we're the star of the team, that the planet revolves around us. That mindset is the perfect breeding ground for pride to worm its way into our hearts.

Instead, we must remind ourselves daily that there's only one star in the kingdom of God, and that's not you or me but Jesus Christ. This changes the temperature of our hearts so that we might walk in humility. Remember, it's not about me, but Jesus!

Truth to Believe

Humility accomplishes infinitely more in my life than pride could ever do. I strive to be a humble servant of the Lord.

33_

forgiveness

The Problem

We struggle to forgive.

When someone wrongs us, hurts us, or betrays our trust, one of the hardest things to do is to forgive that person. And yet that's precisely what Jesus calls us to do. The Bible says that if we refuse to forgive others, how can we expect God to forgive us?

"For if you forgive others their offenses, your heavenly Father will forgive you as well. But if you don't forgive others, your Father will not forgive your offenses" (Matthew 6:14–15 CSB).

The Solution

Forgive quickly, and forgive often.

The world we live in promotes the opposite of Jesus' teachings on forgiveness. Our culture says that if someone wrongs you, then they deserve all the bitterness and resentment you care to throw at them. It's "their own fault." But when we adopt this attitude, not only are we doing the opposite of what Jesus does for us but we're also killing ourselves.

Bitterness and resentment are like drinking poison and expecting your enemy to die from it. It will hurt your soul just as much, if not more, than it will hurt theirs. We're also keeping ourselves from the freedom that comes with forgiveness. We're weighing our own souls down with a weight we were never meant to carry.

The solution is to forgive quickly and often!

Forgiveness doesn't mean that thing they did to you didn't happen. It means that it *stops* happening. It means it's over. The hurt it caused you doesn't have to continue causing you more hurt.

I get it. That sounds radical. I know what it's like to be cut deeply by someone. Are we really called to forgive? The apostle Peter himself struggled to wrap his mind around this issue, which was why, in Matthew, chapter 18, he asked Jesus how many times he should forgive his brother who has hurt him. He even suggests seven times, thinking maybe that might be a good limit to one's forgiveness.

Jesus responds with the instruction to forgive: "I tell you, not seven times, but seventy-seven times" (Matthew 18:22). The number *seven* is a symbolic number in the Bible that signifies "completion" and "spiritual perfection." Jesus tells us to keep forgiving others over and over again, completely, not holding anything back.

Why? Because this is what Jesus does for us.

Think about how many times you've sinned today. Just today. The quick lustful thought. The harsh word said to someone when you were stressed. The greed in your heart as you checked your stock portfolio.

Every time we sin, we break the heart of God. And yet He continues to forgive us, time and time again. We make choices every day that don't reflect our character as sons of God, and yet Jesus doesn't turn His back on us. No! Out of His love and mercy, He forgives us again and again—past, present, and future. That's the kind of forgiveness Jesus offers us.

If you're having a hard time forgiving others today, remember how Jesus has so freely forgiven you. And let this truth set you free from any resentment and bitterness you have toward others.

Next Step Today

You need to find freedom through forgiveness.

Is there anyone in your life you've been withholding forgiveness from or have negative feelings about? Maybe it's someone who either said or did something horrible to you.

Your next step is to call them or meet with them and let them know you've forgiven them. Not in a holier-than-thou way but approaching them with the heart of Jesus: "What you did to me really hurt me. I didn't understand it, but I want you to know I don't hold it against you anymore. In fact, I want to ask for your forgiveness that I didn't forgive you sooner. Will you forgive me?"

It sounds radical, I know. Yet this will lead to a radical level of freedom in your life that can only be found through forgiving those people who have wronged you. Make that call today!

Habit to Work Toward

"Make the predecision to be impossible to offend." I heard someone say this, and it deeply resonated with me.

What if we *predecided* that we wouldn't hold on to the things people said to us but instead chose to have a heart of compassion and understanding?

What if we *predecided* that we would care more about people's souls than about our being right?

Truth to Believe

Although it's hard, I'll do the right thing and forgive others because Jesus keeps on forgiving me.

34_

demons

The Problem

Most people don't believe that demons actually exist.

When you don't believe demons exist, you will end up making demons out of people. You'll make people your enemy instead of the devil. You'll think your neighbor is who you should be watching out for instead of the roaring lion that is seeking to destroy your life.

We must wake up and remember that we have a real enemy, and this is a real battle we're in. The good news is that it's one we can win!

The Solution

Fight the right enemy, and in the right way.

Paul tells us in Ephesians 6:12 that our real enemy is not flesh and blood, but the dark and demonic powers of evil:

> For our struggle is not against flesh and blood, but against the rulers, against the authorities, against the powers of this dark world and against the spiritual forces of evil in the heavenly realms.

It's important that we see the enemy for who he is. Your neighbor is not your enemy; it's the person controlling your neighbor. Your enemy is not your ex. "You don't know my ex," you say. "She has lasers that shoot out of her eyes, and she smites puppies." That's terrifying, but she's still not your enemy. It's the one influencing your ex. It's not the politician who is your enemy; it's the one behind the politician.

Our battle is not against flesh and blood, but against the powers of darkness and the spiritual forces of evil.

We must not confuse the battlefield with our mission field. We're not called to fight people; we're called to reach people for Christ. Instead, we fight the spirits of darkness and the devil, who is the source of evil and who uses deception to lead people astray. But how do we do that?

Paul goes on in Ephesians, chapter 6, urging us to put on the full armor of God. He lists six things: truth, righteousness, peace, faith, salvation, and the Word of God. Notice how none of the things Paul mentions are physical weapons, because you can't fight a supernatural battle with man-made weapons. You need something much greater for this fight.

The takeaway from chapter 6 is not to go to the Facebook comment section and wage war with people who disagree with the teachings of Jesus. The takeaway here is to go sit in your prayer closet with Jesus and wage war against your real enemy. It's to use truth to combat the lies the devil tells you. The takeaway is to push back darkness in your city or town by sharing the gospel with others and living a life that is holy and pleasing to the Lord.

Go win the fight!

Next Step Today

Make sure you've put on the full armor of God.

1. Salvation. Do you know Jesus as the Lord and Savior of your life?
2. Righteousness. Are you pursuing a holy life?
3. Truth. Do you know the actual truth? Do you live the truth?
4. Peace. Peace is not found in a place; it's found in a person: Jesus. Do you have peace? Are you spending time with the person who can give you peace?
5. Faith. It's *impossible* to please God without faith. Do you believe God for the impossible?
6. The Word of God. Paul refers to the Bible as "the sword of the Spirit." It's the weapon we use to attack the lies of the devil. Are you wielding your weapon, or is it collecting dust on the bookshelf?

Your next step today is to go down this list and make sure you have on the *full armor* of God, not just a piece or two. This battle requires that you wear all of it!

Habit to Work Toward

A professional marksman is always checking and rechecking their environment to make sure they have their rifle set on the right spot to increase their chances of hitting the desired target.

As Christians we need to get in the habit of remembering who our enemy is, and what it is he's doing. We're not called to fight our neighbors. We're fighting demons and the devil, who are seeking to destroy our lives.

Truth to Believe

I'm in a fight against the powers of this dark world, the spiritual forces of evil. But with Jesus on my side, I will be victorious!

35_

influence

The Problem

Influence has become an obsession.

In fact, there are many people who want to do things for God more than they want to be with God. The temptation for a lot of young men is to seek influence for God more than they seek to be influenced by God.

We want to speak, but we don't want to listen. We want to post, but we don't want to pray. We desire influence, but we don't want intimacy.

The Solution

The solution is to make Jesus your primary goal.

If intimacy with Jesus is your main goal, you will end up with more kingdom influence than you ever thought possible. The Bible is filled with examples of this.

Daniel had more impact in his prayer closet than the king did on his throne. Joseph had more favor in a prison cell than anyone in his country. Paul had more influence as a tentmaker than any other ministry leader at the time.

If you want to do great things for God, you've got to want God more than you want great things. It is not the influencers who make the greatest impact in the kingdom of God; it's the influenced. Men who allow God to influence every decision, action, plan, and dream. Men who make Jesus their prize.

There was a man in the Bible who came to be known as the "rich young ruler." In Matthew 19, Jesus offers the young man the opportunity of a lifetime: to sell all he has and to come follow Him. Many Bible scholars believe this was an invitation for the man to become the thirteenth disciple, along with Peter, John, James, Matthew, and the others.

What's heartbreaking is that the man rejected Jesus' offer because he would not sell his possessions and give up his status. Why? Because he loved having influence more than he loved being influenced.

Today that man is no longer rich, he is no longer young, and he rules over nothing. Today the disciples who gave up everything to be influenced by Jesus have rewards in heaven, they will live forever, and they reign with Christ.

Real, lasting, eternal purpose and influence comes from one thing: following Jesus closely.

Next Step Today

You can't be influenced if you don't allow Jesus inside enough to change you.

God doesn't need your talents; He wants your submission. God doesn't need your abilities; He wants your full surrender. God doesn't need your influence; He wants your intimacy.

Are you carrying anything today that's keeping you from going "all in" with Jesus? Maybe it's the opinions of others. Maybe it's a bitter heart toward others. Maybe it's your dreams not being aligned with God's will for you.

influence

Whatever it is, your next step today is to make sure that Jesus is truly sitting on the throne of your heart.

Give yourself the rich-young-ruler test. If Jesus approached you today in the flesh and invited you to follow Him and be His disciple, is there anything that He could ask from you that you wouldn't be willing to give up? If so, why?

It could be that very thing that's keeping you from all that God has in store for your life.

Habit to Work Toward

Don't speak for God until you've sat with God.

For instance, don't post about God or lead a Bible study or give encouragement to someone until you've first let God speak to you that day.

This gets you in the habit of being influenced by God before you attempt to influence others for God.

Truth to Believe

Real kingdom impact comes from allowing Jesus to influence me first.

36_

"little sin"

The Problem

We all have our "little sin."

You know, the sin we keep around. The sin we make excuses for. The sin we hide from others. The sin we rationalize, telling ourselves it's not hurting anybody or anything.

The problem with little sin is that it's not going to stay "little" forever. Little sin is killing you.

The Solution

Drag your "little sin" into the light.

There was this man who lived in South Africa. He decided to keep a baby hippo as a pet. Every day he would go out to his backyard and feed the hippo and sit with him for a while. He had this hippo for about five years. Then one morning he went outside to feed his beloved hippo, and that pet hippo dragged his owner into the river and ate him.[1]

Crazy, right? Yet holding on to sin in our lives works just like that baby hippo. It comes disguised as a pet when really it's a predator. And we feed it, and we keep it around, and then one

1. https://www.snopes.com/fact-check/south-african-killed-by-pet-hippo/, accessed October 14, 2024.

day the thing we've been feeding in private begins to feed on us in public.

Little sin kills you. Why? Because there's no such thing as "little sin" to God. Romans 6:23 tells us the consequence of sin is *death*. All sin.

That sin you keep calling "little" is not little at all. And sin is never content to stay the same size. John Owen once said, "You either be killing sin or sin be killing you." So the solution to your sin problem is to get it out of hiding and into the light. The solution is to be killing sin!

There are three ways we can drag our sin into the light and find freedom from it.

1. Confess it to God. This is called *repentance*. It's simply praying to God, confessing your sin, and asking Him to forgive you—which we know He's always faithful to do.
2. Confess it to a brother in Christ. James, chapter 5, tells us that we should confess our sins to each other and pray for each other so that we may be healed. In other words, when you confess your sin to another person, this helps you find freedom from what you've been struggling with.
3. Ask someone to hold you accountable. Find an advocate, someone you can lean on as you begin to eradicate the sin from your life. This is also a person you can call on and confess to again if need be. And someone you can pray with in your battle against sin.

Your sin doesn't have to keep winning the fight. Drag it into the light today.

Next Step Today

Confess your sin to a brother in Christ.

Don't just confess it to anyone. I'd suggest it be someone who fits that description: *a brother in Christ*.

As men it's not wise to confess our sins to a woman, even a sister in Christ. The only woman I confess my sin to is my wife. Why? Because there are lines we shouldn't cross here. Confessing intimate things to someone of the opposite sex, someone who is not your spouse, might lead to all sorts of other sins! It can also lead to emotional ties between you and another person that are unhealthy, distracting you from living a life of holiness.

When you meet with a brother in Christ, not only can you tell him about what you're going through with your personal battle against sin, you can talk to him about your shared goal: to follow Christ faithfully.

I meet with about a dozen men on Monday mornings. We study the Bible together and regularly confess our sins to one another. It's beautiful. We don't do it to wallow in that sin and stay there. We do it because we want to overcome our sin. And our brothers are there to encourage us to do just that—overcome sin.

Habit to Work Toward

Confess your sin to your brother in Christ immediately after it happens. Don't wait!

The less time your sin is hidden in the dark, the better. If/when you sin, a great habit to work toward is to go to God in prayer and repent right away, then confess the sin to your brother in Christ—for accountability and for encouragement to keep fighting "the good fight" (see 2 Timothy 4:7).

Truth to Believe

There is no sin that's too little to avoid any consequences, and there is no sin that's too big for God's healing grace.

37_

radical obedience

The Problem

We care too much about destinations. We care too much about outcomes.

I get it. I'm a control freak. I'm a planner. This chapter was planned. I planned when I was going to write it, where I was going to write it, and if I didn't get to write it today at a certain coffee shop like I planned to, I probably would have been stressed out.

We love plans. God loves steps.

We love outcomes. God loves obedience.

The Solution

Obey God and leave the outcome to Him.

Obedience is your job, and the outcome is God's job.

When you're too focused on the destination and outcome, this causes you to miss out on the journey. It causes you to be so focused on what could go wrong that you miss out on the beautiful opportunity to trust Jesus today.

Matthew 6:26 says, "Look at the birds of the air; they do not sow or reap or store away in barns, and yet your heavenly Father feeds them. Are you not much more valuable than they?"

You know what I've never seen birds do? I've never seen them stressing out about which branch they're going to land on. I've never seen one bird acting fearful over how they're going to pay their "birdlord"—a landlord that's a bird. You know why? Because they're focused only on today. They're concerned only about doing what's needed for today.

That's exactly how we should be following Jesus.

I'm not saying you don't need to make plans or think long-term. I'm simply saying don't let the what-ifs of tomorrow distract you from obeying today.

Eugene Peterson's definition of faithfulness is "long obedience in the same direction." I love that. But before you can have long obedience in the same direction, you must have *short* obedience in the same direction. And before you can have short obedience in the same direction, you've got to be living in obedience today.

Don't overcomplicate following Jesus. You don't need to have your whole life figured out today because you know someone who does! So obey Jesus today, right now. Then go to bed. Wake up tomorrow and obey Jesus again. Then again. Then again.

Before you know it, your obedient days will lead to a faithful, obedient life.

Next Step Today

Stop carrying around the consequences of obedience.

Charles Stanley said, "Obey God and leave the consequences up to God." All those what-ifs and what-abouts—leave those with God! And remember, "If God is for us, who can be against us?" (Romans 8:31).

This prayer has helped me whenever I find myself struggling to be radically obedient:

God, I give up control right now. My life is so much better off in your hands than it is in mine. I trust you fully. I choose to obey because I know you'll bring about the right outcome. Thank you for not just being the way but for showing me the way. Amen.

Habit to Work Toward

Run your decisions through the obedience filter:

1. Does God's Word support my decision?
2. Does the wise counsel of others in my life support this decision?
3. Is this what I sense God is asking me to do?
4. Have I prayed about it?

If still yes, what are you waiting for? Obey!

Truth to Believe

I will never regret radical obedience to Jesus.

38_

do hard things

The Problem

Nobody loves hard things. Nobody loves trials. Nobody loves difficulties.

In fact, most people run the opposite direction when facing difficulty.

We'd much rather be in a good season or a comfortable season. The problem is that when we run from hard things, we're actually running from God and His making us more like Him. We're running from our calling. We're running from God getting glory from our lives.

The Solution

Do hard things.

James said it this way: "Consider it pure joy, my brothers and sisters, whenever you face trials of many kinds, because you know that the testing of your faith produces perseverance. Let perseverance finish its work so that you may be mature and complete, not lacking anything" (James 1:2–4).

James is telling us not to run from the hard things. Instead, we should embrace and even celebrate the opportunity to do hard things because when we do hard things, God is working through us and in us at the same time. We're faced with the opportunity for God to help us overcome those things, but more importantly, we're given the opportunity to become more like Jesus.

One theory for why people never want to do hard things is because we don't like to put ourselves in a position where we might feel pain. In fact, we'd like to avoid pain at all costs. However, I don't think people hate pain so much. I think people hate pain without a purpose.

I've been training for a marathon. My life is full of pain every morning! Today I ran ten miles, and I currently have my left foot in a bucket of ice because it's in pain. But I keep running because I can see the purpose. I can see myself crossing the finish line and completing a goal I've had for a long time.

When the purpose outweighs the pain, you can do hard things.

Romans 8:28 says, "And we know that in all things God works for the good of those who love him, who have been called according to his purpose." Notice how the text says *all things*. Not just the easy things, but all things, and this includes the hard things. Your pain has a purpose. Your hard seasons have a purpose.

God is more concerned with who you are becoming than what you are doing. And if you'll let Him, He is going to use this hard thing or hard season to make you more like Him. That makes the pain worth it, so rejoice.

Next Step Today

If you're in a difficult season, today is the day to reframe how you're thinking about it.

Rather than ask, How can I get out of this?, instead ask, What can I get out of this? What's God trying to do in my life right now? Does this pain have a purpose I can't see because I'm wanting to avoid this hard season? What might happen if I fully surrendered to God in this?

Reframing our approach to hard things will very rarely make them any easier, but it will give us purpose and help us to see God working in our lives, using the hard things to make us more like Him.

Here's a prayer for today:

Dear Father, I may not see what you're doing right now, but I know you're doing something. So today, in the middle of my difficulties, I praise your name and rejoice. You have my best interests in mind, and you're close to me always. I pray that while I'm in this hard season, you'll do the work that needs to happen in my life. Amen.

Habit to Work Toward

Don't run from trials. Instead, rejoice in them.

I have a friend who is known for this. Recently we were flying somewhere together, and our flight had gotten delayed for the third time that day. If it was delayed just one more time, we would not arrive at our destination. This would mean the event I was scheduled to preach at would not have a preacher that night.

My friend's response to this was, "What a beautiful opportunity to trust in Jesus."

Amen. Rejoice. Always.

Truth to Believe

God is working all things for my good—even the hard things.

39_

commit to community

The Problem

Everyone says they want community and yet few people are willing to commit to community. For true, fruitful, and biblical community requires our commitment.

If we want the kind of community where we can be sharpened, encouraged, held accountable, and helped to become the best version of ourselves that we can be, we must be willing to stick with the people in our lives.

As my wife loves to say, "You can't be flaky and faithful at the same time." And you can't have community without commitment.

The Solution:

The Bible has quite a lot to say about community. For example, Hebrews 10:24–25 says, "And let us consider how we may spur one another on toward love and good deeds, not giving up meeting together, as some are in the habit of doing, but encouraging one another—and all the more as you see the Day approaching."

Verse 25 encourages us to not give up on meeting together. Paul is telling us to find good, godly men to do life with and to stick with them. Don't quit when one of you gets on the other's nerves. Don't back out because it's no longer as convenient for you as it was before. Fruit takes time to produce. So does community.

When I was a kid, I went on a camping trip and learned something interesting about campfires. One hot ember left alone in the fire will only burn for a few minutes, but if you put a group of embers together, they can burn for hours or even days.

The same can be said for a community that's committed to one another. If you want to go fast, go alone. If you want to go far, *go together*!

Back to Paul's words in chapter 10 of Hebrews. In verse 24, he tells us to consider how we may *spur* one another on toward love and good deeds. The first way a community spurs one another on is through encouragement, sharpening and helping each other. The word *spur* comes from the concept of a horseback rider digging their heels into the sides of the horse, often painfully, to urge the animal forward.

Paul is saying a community should encourage you, but there's a part of this that means it will also hurt a little. If we choose to be in community only when things are "ten out of ten" with the people in that community, we're missing out on a huge opportunity. The opportunity to become like Christ.

When things are perfect and going great, it's very easy to love your community. But when things start to go sideways, when the cracks start to show and the honeymoon phase of community starts to wear off, that's when we're given the opportunity to spur one another on and STICK with each other, just like Jesus sticks with us.

When we commit to community, we go further than we could on our own. We're also given beautiful opportunities to be formed more in the image of Christ.

Next Step Today

It's easy to fall out of community with people. Being committed to community takes real intentionality and even planning.

Is there someone in your life you've fallen out of community with? Maybe life just got super busy, you lost touch, or you haven't been able to get together like you used to. Today is the day to fight for that friendship!

Pick up the phone and catch up with that person. Or send them a text and ask to get together.

Chances are they've been missing spending time with you too. Let's do the hard work of committing to, and sticking with, community.

Habit to Work Toward

One of the best places to commit to community is at your local church. I have another chapter in this book where I dive into the subject of the church. But a great habit to implement in your life is never to miss back-to-back Sundays at church.

As for our family, we never miss church. Of course, we're the pastors! But even if we weren't, we would do everything possible not to miss a Sunday being in the house of God because that's where our community gets together.

I get it, though. Sometimes there's a valid reason for your not making it to church. Yet that should be the exception, not the rule. Commit to your community.

Truth to Believe

Being a part of a devoted, close-knit community requires both time and consistency.

40_

investing

The Problem

One day you wake up and suddenly you have more money coming into your bank account than you've ever had before.

What? Noah, that doesn't sound like a problem.

It's not. The problem is that many men don't know how to properly invest that money. Instead of putting it to work for their future, they let it sit in a savings account where it collects very little interest, or worse, they spend it.

The Solution

Invest your money wisely and intentionally.

"The plans of the diligent lead to profit as surely as haste leads to poverty" (Proverbs 21:5).

When I got my first full-time job, I was fortunate enough to have some men in my life who were smart about money teach me how to invest. If not for them, financially I'd be in a much different place.

What I've learned is that Proverbs 21:5 is true. Diligent and consistent investing over time leads to an abundance or a profit, whereas hasty and greed-centered investing leads to poverty.

For the last eight years I've invested one time per month in a Fidelity brokerage account, which is an investment account. Every month I do the same exact thing. I buy something called index funds. It's basically one of the safest and most boring investments a person can make. But it works! Today, if you added up all the dollars I put into that account over the last eight years, it's a decent amount of money. Yet that money has been receiving interest and compounding. Eight years later, I have over *double* the amount I invested in this account!

That's the power of consistent investing.

On the flip side of that, I've done some hasty investing. There was one time I heard about a certain type of cryptocurrency that some people claimed was going to take off to the moon in price. I let the emotions and the idea of making lots of money get ahold of me instead of wisdom and rationality, and I bought $500 worth of it. That $500 is currently worth $5. A very poor investment.

There are lots of wise ways to invest your money. The solution is to do it and do it consistently, even if it's only a small amount of money at first. We all can get by with spending a little less and investing a little more. And if we do that, our future selves and our future families will thank us.

Next Step Today

If you aren't already investing, today is the day to start.

A retirement account is a good place to start. I'm no financial guru, but I do have men in my life who are. And according to them, the wisest thing you can do with your money is to make sure you're taken care of in your retirement.

There are a few options to consider. If you work somewhere that offers a 401(k) or a 403(b) or some sort of similar retirement plan, then that's where you should begin investing your money. One reason for this is that employers often match a certain percentage of these funds, which means you'll be getting extra, *free* money!

If you work somewhere that doesn't offer one of those two accounts, you can invest in a retirement account called a Roth IRA, which is what I did. A Roth IRA is simply a bucket you can drop money into every month as an investment. Once you deposit the money into the account, you can then use the money to buy index funds or stocks that will gain interest over time. Roth IRAs are amazing because they will gain interest that's tax-free. Later, when you withdraw that money in retirement, you won't have to pay any taxes on your gains.

So your next step today is to make sure you're investing in your retirement.

Habit to Work Toward

Make investing a habit.

My wife and I invest monthly in our retirement accounts. We've made an investment plan for any extra money that comes in as well.

We invest in our Roth IRA, and any extra gets invested in such things as real estate, a traditional brokerage account, and safer forms of cryptocurrency.

Spend some time researching the different types of investments, learn their pros and cons, and start putting your money to work!

Truth to Believe

Through good financial planning and stewardship, I can make my money work for me instead of the other way around.

41_

pace

The Problem

It's hard to hear from God when your life is too busy to listen.

Dallas Willard, when asked how to follow Jesus well, gave this advice: "You must ruthlessly eliminate hurry from your life."

Why? Because hurry kills intimacy. Hurry kills peace. Hurry kills joy.

Hurry kills *life*.

The Solution

The peace of Jesus is best experienced at the pace of Jesus.

Have the pace of Jesus.

For some of us that means we need to speed up, for Jesus is not pro-laziness. Jesus came with a mission, and He moved with intention. He made the most of His life on earth, and we should too.

For others of us, having the pace of Jesus might mean slowing down. It might mean taking more time off to be with Jesus and our family and friends. It might mean creating more margin in our calendars.

How do we live at Jesus' pace? That's hard to answer specifically for everyone, but here are three guiding principles to get us started:

1. Practice the sabbath or a period of rest.
   Sabbath is the practice of resting one day out of the week. Contrary to popular belief, sabbath does not mean a day to nap—although it could include a nap. Sabbath means a twenty-four-hour period to worship and do things that bring you delight. It means taking twenty-four hours to stop producing and simply trust that God is your provider and sustainer. When done right, the sabbath will become your favorite day of the week!

2. Work hard during the week.
   Sabbath should feel different from the other six days of the week. It shouldn't feel like every other day because the other days you are working hard to do things with excellence. Whether that's your schoolwork or your job, we as Christians are called to do things well.
   Colossians 3:23 says, "Whatever you do, work at it with all your heart, as working for the Lord, not for human masters." If our work is being done in the name of the Lord, then we should do it well and with excellence.

3. Keep Jesus first.
   Is your life currently moving at a pace where Jesus can interrupt it? Do you have time set aside each day to sit with Jesus, or does He regularly get pushed to the next day? If you don't have time for a few uninterrupted moments with Jesus, it's highly unlikely you're living life at His pace.
   Check your pace. Adjust your pace. Enjoy time with Jesus.

Next Step Today

Do a "pace check."

Do you need to speed up? Do you need to slow down? Do you find yourself wasting time? Do you find yourself constantly strapped for time?

It's probably time for a pace adjustment.

Today is a great day to go for a fifteen-minute walk. Go outside—with no music or other distractions, making sure your phone has been silenced—just you and God and a walk. Get honest with yourself and with God. What pace do you need to adjust to?

Habit to Work Toward

In my book *Holy Habits*, I do a deep dive into what my weekly sabbath looks like. I'd encourage you to check out this resource because I believe everyone should practice a weekly sabbath.

My sabbath typically includes sleeping in, spending the morning with my family, eating great food, playing some golf, and going on a date with my wife. It also includes spending time with Jesus throughout the day—refueling my soul with Him, spending time with my favorite people, and doing my favorite things.

The way I spend my sabbath causes me to live the other six days of the week differently.

Start practicing a weekly sabbath.

Truth to Believe

One way I can experience the peace of Jesus is by living each day at His pace.

42

learn from everyone

The Problem

As men who are tempted every day with the option to be prideful, it's easy to stop learning.

Eventually we just think we know. We think we know how things work. We think we know why people do what they do. We think we know how the world works.

This is a lie. The truth is we always have something more to learn.

When we stop becoming learners, we stop becoming leaders. Our world needs men who never stop learning—from everyone.

The Solution

Realize you can learn something from everyone. That's right, everyone.

Proverbs 12:15 says, "The way of fools seems right to them, but the wise listen to advice." A wise man listens to advice. A wise man chooses to learn.

Some of my favorite people to learn from are those who are doing what I want to do, and they're doing it well. If you're a new business owner, there are things you could learn from someone who has been a successful business owner for the last twenty-plus years. If you're a college basketball player, a professional athlete could teach you a thing or two about your sport.

A mentor is a great person to learn from. In today's world, you can be mentored by people you've never even met. You can read a book, you can listen to a podcast, or you can watch videos on the internet and gain knowledge and understanding that way. We can learn from mentors at a distance, or we can learn from mentors in person, face-to-face. And we can learn something from everyone. Every interaction with people, good and bad, is an opportunity for us to grow.

Don't make the mistake of thinking you have it all figured out. Always be learning.

Learn how to treat people well when you see someone treat people poorly. Take note of how the elderly man opens the door for his wife at the restaurant. Notice how that person at church made you feel when they remembered your name. Wake up each morning with this attitude: I'm going to learn today!

When we approach life with the attitude of a learner, not only do we practically get better but we spiritually get better too because we're living a life of humility.

Pride says, I've got it all figured out. Humility says, I've got a lot to learn.

Be a learner.

Next Step Today

If you can't remember what you've learned, you probably won't put into practice what you learned.

Your next step is to create a system to help you remember what you're learning. I'm going to share mine with you, but remember, the right system is the one that works for you.

I use the Notes app on my phone. I have a folder labeled BRAIN DUMP. Whenever I hear an interesting quote, watch something inspiring, or learn *anything*, I write it down as a note in this folder. Sometimes I quickly write it, and other times I voice-text the note into the folder. That's all I do with it then.

Once a month I'll go through and sort the notes from the past month into categories. I have about twenty-five categories that describe my notes. Everything from ideas for sermons, things to implement in my marriage, parenting tips, social-media inspiration, and much more. I take all the notes from BRAIN DUMP, and I sort them into new folders.

Now here's where it gets fun.

The next time I need a date-night idea and I can't think of anything, I go to that folder. The next time I need a fresh idea for a sermon, I go to that folder. The next time someone asks me if I have any parenting ideas for a kid who won't listen, I just go to that folder.

Over time my folders have grown exponentially—and so has my knowledge.

Create a system today so that you can implement what you learn from everyone.

Habit to Work Toward

Create margin in your calendar once a month to sort out what you've learned.

No matter what your system for collecting what you've learned is, you're going to need time to sort through it all. This should be fun! Grab a coffee, turn on your favorite playlist, and give yourself time to grow.

Truth to Believe

I have something to learn from everyone.

43_

holiness

The Problem

Godly men are weak when godly men are worldly.

The problem is that so few men are intentionally pursuing holiness. We've fallen for the lie that we can love Jesus and look like the world. We've believed in a false gospel that says we can accept Christ and nothing about our lives need change.

The problem is that we're meant to live as holy men, but we're settling as worldly boys.

The Solution

"Be holy, because I am holy" (1 Peter 1:16).

We're called to the intentional pursuit of holiness. Notice I didn't say *perfection*. You are going to fail. No matter how hard you try, and no matter how good your intentions are, there are going to be days and moments where you fall short. The good news is that Jesus offers His grace to you in those moments so that you can get back up.

You can get back up and continue to pursue holiness.

For whatever reason, there's a stigma surrounding the word *holiness* that is based on a falsehood. When most people hear someone mention holiness, they think of legalism. They think *no fun*. They imagine a long list of rules they must follow.

But that's not holiness.

Two thousand years ago, when people heard the word *holy*, they didn't think such things. What they thought was closer to what we think about when we hear words like *beautiful*, *blessed*, and *set apart for a purpose*. They realized that holiness included a mandate to say no to certain things or behaviors, yet this was always because God had a better *yes* in mind for their lives, a higher purpose.

The same is true for us today. Pursuing holiness doesn't make you legalistic. Holiness makes you like Christ. And that's the kind of men we should aim to be!

Also, we don't pursue holiness to be saved; we pursue holiness because we've been saved. This isn't something we do to earn God's love, favor, or acceptance. We already have His love and acceptance. Holiness is something we seek because we love God in return, and we want what He wants for our lives.

We pursue holiness because we have a new identity in Christ, and with His help we will become more like Him each day.

Next Step Today

Have you made the decision for yourself to pursue holiness?

If not, then today is the day to make that decision. The Bible says that when we accept Christ, the old passes away because the *new* has come. What old things do you need to let pass away so that you can allow the Holy Spirit to make you new?

Maybe your next step is as simple as stopping to hang out in those places that tempt you to be the old you. Maybe it's as simple as refusing to go to that bar or that house where you tend to make decisions you regret.

Maybe your next step is cleaning up your Spotify playlist to reflect the values of holiness that you care about. That might seem like a small thing, but I promise you it will yield massive results. We can't expect to take into our minds and hearts unholy lyrics with unholy messages, then turn around and live a holy life.

Maybe your next step today is to remove whatever temptations you've kept around in your life that make it harder for you to pursue holiness.

Holiness is worth the fight!

Habit to Work Toward

Put a passcode on your content.

It's possible to create passcodes on your content so that you can't watch a movie or a show that has a certain audience rating. You can do this where you don't know the passcode, but your spouse or friend does. That way, anytime you want to watch something that might encourage an unholy lifestyle, you first have to ask them for the passcode and talk over any content issues.

Accountability is a great habit to practice in your pursuit of holiness.

Truth to Believe

I'm called to live a holy life. I do this in obedience to God's Word, and out of my love for Him.

44_

college

The Problem

So many people waste their college years.

They waste college doing things they eventually regret doing. They waste their college years caring about things they will never care about again. They waste college by investing in the wrong relationships. They waste college by not approaching college intentionally with the right goals.

They waste college by making it about themselves instead of making it about Jesus.

The Solution

Make the most out of college.

If I could go back in time and give my incoming-freshman self some advice about college, this is what I would say: stop caring so much about stuff that you won't care at all about when you graduate.

When I was in college, I spent so much time caring about things like fraternity leadership positions, intramural championships, and what people thought of me. What I should have been thinking about was preparing myself for the real world, investing in good friendships, and my relationship with God.

1. Approach college with a long-term mindset, not a four-year one.
2. Stop wasting so much time.
   College is the *prime* season in which to waste time. Video games, parties, and oversleeping all run rampant in college. Something else that runs rampant is people claiming they're "so busy." I promise you, as a thirty-year-old man with a family, a church, and several other responsibilities, your life will only get busier.

   Here's the truth about college: you may be busy, but you're not *that* busy. Stop wasting your time. Get good at managing and making the most of your time. If you're intentional regarding the next four years and how you spend your time, you'll have a big head start on the rest of the students on campus.
3. Find a local church and serve there.
   Don't be flaky about church attendance. Don't be someone who just hops around and never establishes roots. Find a church you like and go all in! Serve. One of my biggest regrets is not doing this. When you find a great church and commit to it, you open yourself up to so many blessings. You will experience the obvious benefits such as spiritual growth and discipleship training, but you'll also find a new family, people to encourage you in your walk with God.
4. Don't date unless you're looking to get married.
   If you want to date, go ahead and do so. But, like I said earlier in chapter 13, my advice is to not date until you can see yourself getting married in the next year. If you date before you're ready for marriage, you're setting yourself up for all kinds of heartbreak. You might

welcome to manhood

experience relational heartbreak with your girlfriend, or you could experience God's heart breaking if you allow that relationship to cross boundaries sexually.

Be friends instead. Hang out in groups. Pray that your future spouse will enter your life at the right time.

Next Step Today

Whether you're in college/university now or heading there soon, I would suggest sitting down and thinking through what your goals are. I'm not just talking about your academic goals, although those should probably be a part of this. I'm talking about your spiritual, personal, and relational goals.

When you graduate in four years, who do you want to be? What do you want to be known for? What do you want to have accomplished from your time spent in college? It's really hard to meet a goal unless you've clearly defined it beforehand.

Write out your goals and reverse engineer them. What needs to happen your freshman year for you to stay on track? Sophomore? Junior? Senior?

Approach college with the end (graduation) in mind. These years go by fast. Don't waste them.

Habit to Work Toward

Share your college goals with someone who doesn't go to school with you, a nonstudent like a parent, a mentor, or an accountability partner.

Ask them if they will check in on you and ask how you're doing in reaching these goals. A good time for checking in is after each semester.

Truth to Believe

College is not a season to waste, but a season to approach with intentionality and personal goal setting.

45_

closed doors

The Problem

Doors close.

We plan, we get excited, we get our hopes up . . . only for the doors to slam in our faces. One of the most frustrating and discouraging things in life is when you're sure a door—a relationship, a job, an opportunity—is the right one for you to step through, but then you see it close and you're proven to be wrong.

When a door closes, we have a choice to make. We can let the closed door stop us in our tracks, or we can leave the door behind and go knock on a new or different door.

The Solution

Celebrate when doors close.

Yes, that's right—celebrate.

Romans 8:28 says, "We know that in all things God works for the good of those who love him, who have been called according to his purpose." If that be the case, then our facing a closed door in our lives is no different.

I've come to learn that what looks like rejection is often God's protection. Every time God gave me a *no*, it was followed up by a better *yes*. Here's a truth you may need to hear today: God loves you too much to give you everything you think you want.

God knows you better than you know yourself, His ways are higher than your ways, and as much as you care about the details of your life, God actually cares more.

Sometimes it takes weeks, months, or even years, but eventually, when we look back on the closed doors, we can see the purpose of their closing—even the most difficult ones we had to come to grips with. So if you feel as though you've gotten a *no* recently, be encouraged that God knows what He's doing. Always.

Why should you celebrate when a door closes? Because a better door is going to open, a door God will hold open for you to step through. I'd much rather have to wait a little while longer for God's plan to unfold versus marching ahead of Him on my own. The old adage holds true: "The only thing more difficult than waiting on God is wishing that you had."

When a door closes, celebrate it, and trust that God is right there with you. Remember Romans 8:28.

Next Step Today

Move on from your closed doors.

One reason God may not be doing a new thing in your life is because you keep picking up the old things.

Maybe it's a relationship. You've been broken up, or you keep breaking up and getting back together, only for nothing to change. Let this be your sign. Put your trust in God and let the door close completely.

Maybe it's the disappointment of not getting the job you so wanted. It's okay to be disappointed; just don't let your disappointment turn into defeat. It could be that a month from now, you'll be thanking God that He didn't let you get that job because an even better one came your way!

Let the door close. Mourn if you need to. But then get back up and start believing God to be faithful, just like He's always been to you.

Habit to Work Toward

Look back, and often.

Whenever I need my faith strengthened, I look back on the past seasons of my life when I really needed God to come through for me.

I reflect on when the woman I thought I was going to marry broke up with me and remember that God had another plan worked out the entire time. I think about when COVID-19 hit right as I was going on the road full-time, preaching at events, and all my events got canceled . . . only for God to work out every detail.

Sometimes when we're in a closed-door situation, all we need do is look back at the last season of closed doors and remind ourselves of God's faithfulness and goodness during that season. Remember, He's the same yesterday, today, and forever. He's always looking out for us, for we are His sons.

Look back, be encouraged, and put your faith and trust in Him!

Truth to Believe

When God closes a door, I can be sure it's for my good and that He's watching out for me.

46_

king chasing > dream chasing

The Problem

For a long time now, there's been this false teaching going around called the "prosperity gospel," which many unfortunately believed in and still do to this day. The main concept behind the prosperity gospel says that if you follow Jesus, you will in turn receive lots of financial blessings.

Most recently this prosperity gospel has morphed into another false gospel that I call the "dream gospel."

Those who believe in the dream gospel claim that if you follow Jesus, He will in turn help you realize all your dreams. The problem with this false teaching is that (a) it's not true and/or biblical; and (b) if you believe this, you'll end up following your dreams and not following Jesus.

The Solution

Fall more in love with Jesus than with your dreams coming true.

But, Noah, doesn't the Bible say that God will give me the desires of my heart?

No. Actually the Bible says, "Take delight in the LORD, and he will give you the desires of your heart" (Psalm 37:4). Notice there is an instruction at the beginning of the verse: "Take delight in the LORD . . ." This means to find your joy in Him first, to find your identity in Him first, to find your purpose in Him first—to put God first in all things! And *then* God will give you the desires of your heart.

The order here matters and makes all the difference.

For many of us, the temptation is to run after our dreams while sprinkling some Jesus into the mix. But Jesus is not your sidekick. Don't follow your dream and use Jesus. Instead, follow Jesus and use your dream!

Okay, Noah, but I know lots of people who have put Jesus first, and their dreams still didn't come true. What do you have to say about that?

I know people like that too. And out of all the ones who have truly put Jesus first in their lives, not even one of them would say they regret it. Something profound happens when you fall more in love with Jesus than you do with your dreams: your dreams begin to change. Your desires begin to change. The things you want to accomplish in your life begin to change. Why? Because when you fall in love with someone, you start to care about what they care about.

True purpose doesn't come from building your dreams. True purpose comes from building God's dreams.

You might be reading this and have a dream in mind. That's great. Fall in love with Jesus and go after that dream! There's a good chance God put that dream inside of you, and you might just accomplish it and be given the amazing opportunity of giving God the glory through your dream.

But there's also a good chance that you fall in love with Jesus and your dream doesn't come true. You don't accomplish what you were hoping for. Yet something even better could happen to you then: God could give you a new dream, one that will allow you to be obedient to the King.

Chase the King, and let Him show you what to dream.

Next Step Today

Fall in love with the King.

What caused me to initially fall in love with Jesus was hearing what He had to say. Most Bibles make this especially easy to see or read because they emphasize the words of Jesus by using red ink.

I challenge you to open your Bible today to the book of John and read the words printed in red. It should only take you about fifteen minutes to go through the entire book. But take your time as you do it! Think about the words Jesus spoke, paying special attention to what He said about His mission on earth, His desires, His care and love for you.

When you meditate on the words of Jesus, you realize how wonderful it is that we have such a king as Jesus. A king so easy to fall in love with, and one who is madly in love with us.

Habit to Work Toward

The most beautiful prayer of all time is "The Lord's Prayer." This can be found in the Gospel of Matthew, where Jesus teaches us how to pray. Jesus later directs this prayer to God the Father, submitting himself completely to His Father's will: "Your kingdom come, your will be done, on earth as it is in heaven . . ." (Matthew 6:9–13).

The Lord's Prayer is the supreme example of what it looks like to submit ourselves to the King instead of to our dreams. As you chase your dreams, a good habit to develop is to pray these simple yet powerful words. Before you start the business meeting: "Your kingdom come, your will be done." Before you step into the classroom or onto the playing field: "Your kingdom come, your will be done."

Remind yourself regularly that you'd lay your dream at the feet of Jesus if He asked you to.

Truth to Believe

My King is more beautiful than my dream.

47_

bounce back

The Problem

Even though we are choosing to step fully into manhood, we're going to fail sometimes.

We're going to fall short. We're going to blow it. We're going to sin.

The problem is that many people allow their failures to cause them to believe that they themselves are failures. We allow our mistakes to cause us to think we are mistakes.

We allow our sin to keep us from continuing to follow Jesus and become more like Him.

The Solution

Not long ago I bought my son, Lion, his first ice cream cone. It was a magical experience. As you can imagine, he *loved* it.

By the time he was finished with his vanilla treat, it was quite literally all over his entire body. He had ice cream in his hair, all over his face, and all over his clothes. He kept trying to wipe the ice cream off his face, but because he had it on his hands, he only made things worse. What Lion needed was his dad to clean him up—who didn't have ice cream all over himself.

There are a lot of people who have found themselves in a mess, and they're trying hard to clean themselves up—through self-help methods, sheer willpower, or some sort of spirituality that's not based on the Bible. Ultimately, however, *real* change and *real* cleanup must come from someone who is not in a mess themself. This is why the gospel is so powerful. That a holy God would send His Son to earth—who has never sinned and who has no mess to deal with—to clean up our mess by dying on the cross for us, taking the punishment for our sins upon himself. This is the message of the cross: Jesus did what we could never do on our own. He cleaned us up.

And He continues to clean us up. When we fall short and sin after we've repented and accepted Jesus, we still don't have the power to clean ourselves up. Only Jesus can do that! So instead of allowing that sin to cause us to grow weary in following Jesus, or cause us to put ourselves in a "spiritual time-out," we should bounce back up and get in the presence of God.

Proverbs 24:16 says, "For though the righteous fall seven times, they rise again." The number *seven* here indicates that the righteous person will fall a lot. Like all the time. It's a number that speaks of a multitude. So the author of this proverb is telling us, you are going to fall! But because you have been made righteous through the finished work of Jesus Christ on the cross, you can get back up. You can bounce back.

What do you do when you fail? You ask Jesus for His forgiveness. You repent of your sin immediately. You thank God that He's promised never to give up on you, never to leave or turn His back on you. And then you bounce back. You get back up!

You keep following Jesus.

Next Step Today

Call Dad.

The devil loves to heap shame on us when we do the things we know we shouldn't do. The problem with shame is that it keeps us from doing the very thing we should be doing when we fail/sin: bounce back.

I like to put it this way:

Shame: I messed up. Dad's gonna kill me.
Gospel: I messed up. I need to call Dad.

This beautifully paints the picture of how we need to rewire our brains when it comes to shame and forgiveness. Jesus does not want you to carry shame today. He wants you to call Him, to talk to Him, and to let Him forgive you.

Instead of walking in shame with your head down and beating yourself up, go call Dad.

Habit to Work Toward

We want to build the habit of calling Dad quickly. We also want to build the habit of calling others quickly—asking for forgiveness when we've wronged someone.

Don't let your mistakes ruin your friendships and relationships. Be the first one to ask for forgiveness. Drop your pride and do what's right. Bounce back!

Truth to Believe

Because of the grace and mercy of Jesus Christ, when I mess up, I can get back up.

48_

disagreeing well

The Problem

A lot of men only know how to get along with other men who agree with them.

Today disagreeing means hate, and agreeing means love. This is a lie. As men we are called to speak the truth in love, to walk in grace and in truth.

The problem is that we don't know how to disagree well.

The Solution

Jesus didn't tell us to love only those people who love us back.

If that's all you can do, you're not being like Jesus—you're being like everyone else. Jesus said, "Love your enemies and pray for those who persecute you" (Matthew 5:44).

That means loving the one who voted differently from you is the bare minimum. That means loving the person who annoys you on social media is the bare minimum. That means loving the person who wrongs you is the bare minimum. But we can do much more than the bare minimum!

We can follow the example of Jesus.

But how? Jesus was known for speaking the truth always, even if this meant disagreeing with those He was speaking to. Yet He never spoke the truth with a hateful or condemning attitude. He always did so out of His great love.

It's tempting to be either all grace or all truth, or to be either all hate or all love. Yet Jesus' example shows us how to speak the truth while still loving people.

When I was in college, I had a roommate who cared enough about me to have a really hard conversation about something I'd done that wasn't right. He risked disagreeing with me to tell me the truth. And to be honest, I didn't take it very well. My pride was hurt, and I immediately got defensive of my actions and was offended that he would call me out like that.

For about a week our relationship was extremely strained. Not because of my roommate, but because of me. I continued to feel offended and avoided him as much as possible. But my roommate did the opposite. He treated me just like he always had. He continued to be a great friend to me. I came home to our apartment one evening that week to find him cutting the grass, even though that was my responsibility and not his.

Though he spoke the truth to me, he never stopped loving me like a brother. Eventually I came to see that the truth he told me was just that, truth, and that he only shared it because he loved me.

That's the kind of men we should be! Don't speak the truth to people and bounce on them. Don't disagree and let it fracture your relationships. Disagree well. Disagree and love people through it!

Next Step Today

Is there anyone in your life you've disagreed with poorly? Maybe it isn't even your fault. Regardless, today is the day to seek peace with that person.

In Matthew 5:9, Jesus says, "Blessed are the peacemakers, for they will be called children of God."

We're called to be peacemakers. This means *we* go make peace. *We* take the initiative to restore relationships. *We* go first when it comes to doing the hard thing, dropping our pride and working to figure out a way to disagree well.

We don't have to agree with people on everything to love them. We love them no matter what our differences happen to be. Because that's what we're called to do—love people.

Who do you need to make peace with today?

Habit to Work Toward

Another of my favorite Scriptures is Romans 12:10, which tells us to outdo each other in showing honor: "Be devoted to one another in love. Honor one another above yourselves."

Basically, Paul is saying to make a competition out of showing honor to each other. This means never speaking poorly of others. To go out of your way in speaking well of others, even those you disagree with.

Can you imagine what a powerful impact it would have if we, collectively as men, took up the habit of honoring those we disagree with? Rather than focus on where we differ so strongly with people, we decide to speak well of them and the things we admire about them.

This could literally change the world!

Truth to Believe

Jesus demonstrated that it's possible to disagree with people and still love them. I want to follow His example.

49_

how to be great

The Problem

Many of us have the wrong definition of *greatness*.

We measure greatness by how much money we have, how many people know us, and how good we are at what we do. The problem is that Jesus had a completely different definition of greatness. He said, "Anyone who wants to be first must be the very last, and the servant of all" (Mark 9:35).

The world says that greatness is found in status and achievements, but Jesus teaches us that greatness is found in serving others.

The Solution

Direct your desire to be great at the right things.

In chapter 9 of the Gospel of Mark, the disciples are arguing over who is the greatest. Jesus doesn't rebuke them for wanting to be great. He rebukes them for how they were trying to be great.

The disciples didn't have a bad desire for greatness. The disciples had a bad definition of greatness. They were pursuing greatness in the wrong places.

how to be great

Are you pursuing greatness in the wrong places? Are you pursuing it in places like building a platform for yourself? Increasing your bank account? Gaining a job title or an award of achievement? While these things aren't bad in themselves, they don't make you great.

So how do we become great? By serving others. Think about it. You are never more like Jesus than when you're serving others. "Just as the Son of Man did not come to be served, but to serve . . ." (Matthew 20:28).

Jesus was the greatest man of all time, and He also was the greatest *servant* of all time. Jesus served both the rich and the poor. He served the sinners and the saints. He served those who knew who He was and those who didn't have a clue.

Worldly greatness asks, "How can I win?" But greatness in the kingdom of God asks, "Who can I serve?"

When we get to heaven one day, we'll probably be surprised at seeing God give such great rewards to such unknown disciples. People who weren't famous by the world's standards, who didn't have much wealth or status or many accomplishments. But they were great because of their service. They spent their time on earth looking for ways to help people, putting others above themselves.

Martin Luther King Jr. once said, "Anybody can be great because anybody can serve." We all can serve, and those of us who choose to do so are headed for greatness!

Next Step Today

Serve somebody who can give you nothing in return.

After the passage of Scripture I referenced earlier, in Mark 9, Jesus then takes a little child in his arms and says to His disciples, "Whoever welcomes one of these little children in my name welcomes me" (v. 37).

While Jesus clearly loves children, His point here was more about what children represented. A child can give you nothing in return. They can't pay you because they have no money, and children certainly can't elevate your status in the world, as they lack power and influence. Jesus was saying we should serve those who cannot repay us in any way. It's still important to serve everyone, but a true servant seeks to serve others because of what he can do for them, not because of what he might get in return.

Who are the people you can serve today who can't repay you? Maybe it's someone who doesn't have the money to repay you. Maybe it's a stranger you'll never see again. Find someone in need and serve them just because you want to be more like Jesus. This is love in action.

Habit to Work Toward

Serve anonymously.

One of the best ways to serve someone without the person repaying you is to do it anonymously. Something I do occasionally is to pay for the person's coffee who's sitting in the car behind me at the drive-through. Or I pay for someone's meal at a restaurant, someone I don't know. It's one way to keep your heart in the right place, serving another without there being any chance you'll be repaid or given credit for it.

This habit doesn't have to be financial either. I have a dear friend who owns a landscaping business, and he regularly mows people's lawns without payment, just to be a blessing to them.

Go and serve. And don't tell anyone you're doing it. You'll never regret it.

Truth to Believe

Greatness is found in my being a servant to others.

50_
value

The Problem

Our value is constantly under attack.

The devil wants us either to overvalue ourselves or to undervalue ourselves.

Our enemy is at work trying to get us to buy into our own hype and become prideful. Or he's trying to get us to devalue ourselves by thinking poorly about who we are. We must fight both!

The Solution

Know your true value.

There are three key questions you can ask about anything *and* anyone to determine their value:

1. Who made it?
   The most expensive paintings are not always the most beautiful. These are the paintings created by the most esteemed artists. The identity of the artist determines how much money people are willing to pay for the art.

You were made by God the Master Artist. The Bible says in Psalm 139:14 that you were "fearfully and wonderfully made" by Him, the Creator of the universe.

2. How many are there?

The fewer there are, the more valuable. The more there are, the less valuable.

This concept is one we're all familiar with. It's the reason a Toyota is a lot cheaper than a Ferrari. It's why a professional baseball player's rookie trading card is worth more than any of their subsequent seasons. Because there's only one rookie year.

God made only one of you. There are no duplicates. He wired you uniquely and formed you in your mother's womb for such a time as this. The Master Artist made you a "one of one."

3. How much is someone willing to pay?

When my family and I moved to Nashville, we had a hard time trying to purchase a house. Every time we tried to buy one, someone else would outbid us. Buyers were paying extremely high prices for homes at the time.

Frustrated, I met with our real-estate agent and asked him why these people were paying $100,000 or more over the asking price. In my opinion, the houses were definitely not worth that. I'll never forget his response. "Noah, I know this is hard to hear, but a home is worth what someone is willing to pay for it."

The same can be said about people—you're worth what someone is willing to pay. The Bible says that God thought so much of you that He was willing to pay for you with His only Son's life. That He loved and valued you so much that He paid it ALL.

If you've ever questioned your value, remember this: you were made by the Master Artist, you're a one-of-one creation, and you were paid for at the highest price imaginable.

Next Step Today

One of the surest ways to devalue something is to compare it to something else. We devalue ourselves when we compare ourselves to other men.

Comparison is a toxic habit.

Is there anyone in your life you are regularly comparing yourself with? Can you see how this habit is hurting your own sense of worth? I would challenge you to remind yourself of the truth by declaring the statement below today. Read it out loud, and believe it:

I am fearfully and wonderfully made. I don't have to do anything to become valuable because God showed me my value by laying down His life for me. I don't have to earn His love because He gives it freely to me. I am a "one of one," and I was made by the Master Artist. I'm not a mistake. I'm a new creation. I have value because I have Jesus.

Habit to Work Toward

One area where I find myself questioning my own value is when I'm on social media. There are certain accounts and things I see that leave me doubting my value.

A great habit to implement is to approach social media with self-awareness. Are there people or accounts you follow online that cause you to doubt your value? Could you unfollow them or possibly mute their account so that you don't see their posts as much?

The apostle Paul challenges us in 2 Corinthians 10:5 to "take captive every thought to make it obedient to Christ." And my thoughts tend to run rampant on social media. As men in Christ, let's all remember our true value.

Truth to Believe

My value was proven by what God was willing to pay for me and my salvation.

51_

grow there

The Problem

It doesn't take a rocket scientist to understand that the world we live in is getting darker and darker. It seems as though with every passing day, more and more people are turning away from the teachings of Jesus and settling for what this world has to offer.

The problem is that, as we watch this happening in real time, we can become extremely discouraged by it all.

It can feel as though we're losing the fight.

The Solution

Some years ago, I came across an interesting article about Elon Musk and his goal of sending human beings to Mars. Musk has stated publicly that he wants to plant a garden on Mars someday. The reason he wants to do this is because he believes a photograph of the garden, sent back to Earth for everyone to marvel at, would go a long way toward inspiring the next generation of smart, courageous, and bold people to want to travel to Mars. They would be blown away when they saw in the photo something growing where it shouldn't be able to grow, which would in turn light a fire under them to become involved in the Mars program.[1]

As our world grows ever darker, real men, men of God, will have the opportunity to shine brighter. You were made to grow there; you were made to thrive in such a time as this. God knew what our world would be going through today, and He chose you to be a part of the solution. The problem is that we live in a dark world. The solution, though, is that God sent us to shine His light in the midst of the darkness.

"No one lights a lamp and puts it under a basket, but rather on a lampstand, and it gives light for all who are in the house. In the same way, let your light shine before others, so that they may see your good works and give glory to your Father in heaven" (Matthew 5:15–16 CSB).

Don't hide your light. Talk about Jesus with others, and don't be shy. Don't back down because of fear or worry. The Holy Spirit will give you all the courage and boldness you need. Remember Jesus' words: "Whoever acknowledges me before others, I will also acknowledge before my Father in heaven" (Matthew 10:32).

Lots of other men will be watching you as you step fully into manhood, and they'll be inspired to do the same, to follow your example.

The world can look bleak sometimes, but you were made to grow there.

Next Step Today

Congratulations, you've nearly made it to the end of this book. You aren't just a starter; you're a finisher.

---

1. Doug Bierend, "SpaceX Was Born Because Elon Musk Wanted to Grow Plants on Mars," *VICE Digital*, July 17, 2014, https://www.vice.com/en/article /spacex-is-because-elon-musk-wanted-to-grow-plants-on-mars/

If this book helped you in any way, would you consider sharing that with a friend? I'm not asking this because I'm trying to make money or for some sort of selfish gain. I'm asking because, like you, I deeply desire to see men of God stand up and be all that God has called them to be.

A simple next step could be to buy this book for your brother, your friend, or your coworker.

Another step could be to invite another man you'd like to run this race with to a coffee meeting and talk with him about a few of the chapters in the book that challenged you. We're all on this journey of manhood together. Let's be men who are known for helping other men reach their full potential.

Habit to Work Toward

Revisit these ideas and chapters.

I've found that whenever I become complacent in some area of my life, I often regress in that area shortly thereafter. We've got to stay hungry, and we've got to stay humble. We'll never fully "arrive" but must keep fighting such things as apathy, lust, pride, and greed.

We have to keep fighting. We have to keep growing!

Truth to Believe

God created me to be the man of God my world needs.

52

when God seems far away

The Problem

When we perform poorly, God can feel distant from us.

When as men we fall short and fail, it can seem as if God is a million miles away. We subconsciously live our lives like this:

Perform well → Then God will be near → Then I will be loved by God

Therefore, when we don't perform well, not only does it feel as though God is far away, but it feels like God doesn't love us. This a lie, of course, and it's destructive in our pursuit to become the men God has called us to be.

The Solution

Lately I've been potty-training a two-year-old, and it's been a *wild* ride. The other day we were together at a quiet restaurant, and my son began yelling, "I'M POOPING, DAD! I'M DOING IT!" The problem was that we weren't even close to *when God seems far away*

the restroom as he was yelling this. As you can imagine, that dinner was an adventure!

Another time my son had an accident at home. He was rushing to his "big-boy potty" but didn't quite make it before he had to go. Immediately he was overwhelmed with shame. His lower lip began to quiver, his eyes welled up with tears, and he ran and hid in our kitchen pantry.

It broke my heart. I sat outside the pantry door, talking to him and trying to persuade him to come out. I wanted my son to know that even when he performs poorly, I'm not going anywhere.

How would your life change if you truly believed that even when you perform your poorest, your heavenly Father doesn't go anywhere? That even when you feel like locking yourself in the kitchen pantry, God isn't going to give up on you? I think it would be the thing that changes your life!

Again, many of us often live like this:

Perform well → Then God will be near → Then I will be loved by God

But the truth is this:

I'm already loved by God → He will always be near to me → This revelation helps me to perform well

The solution is to flip the script, to focus more on falling in love with Jesus than on trying to perform well. Your performance is always going to fall short, while God's performance will never fall short or fail. He is perfect, righteous, and holy, and He is madly in love with you.

Real transformation begins to happen in our lives when we fall back in love with Him.

Want to perform well as a man? Want to be all that God has made you to be? Fall in love with Jesus.

Next Step Today

There's a concept I first learned by listening to former University of Alabama head football coach Nick Saban and what he called the "1 percent rule." It's the idea that if I can get 1 percent better each day, eventually I'm going to be an entirely different person.

Sometimes when we look far ahead at who we want to become, the difference between who we are right now and who we want to be can feel so daunting that we question whether we'll ever become that man. But if we take a step back and approach our goals while applying the 1 percent rule, those goals become more realistic.

The goal for all of us should be this: *God, help me fall more in love with you by 1 percent today.*

Little by little, day by day, we aim to fall more in love with Him. But how do we do that? We do it by practicing what we already know! We do it by reflecting on the things discussed in this book and working to put them into practice. We do it by reminding ourselves of God's goodness and mercy toward us, His great love, and the miracle of our salvation. We do it by sitting with Jesus, spending time with Him daily.

Your next step today and every day: fall a little bit more in love with Jesus.

Habit to Work Toward

Here's something I recently began doing that may seem cheesy or insignificant but has actually been helpful, which I'd encourage you to try: set a reminder on your phone for every day at the same time that asks the question, *Did you fall more in love with Jesus today?*

It's a simple question, and yet every day at 4:00 p.m., I'm reminded of the goal of this life. I'm reminded of the main thing that will help me become the man I want to be.

Truth to Believe

I already have God's unmerited favor and love, and that is what allows me to perform well.

acknowledgments

Maddy—You're still my favorite everything. Thank you for bringing out the best in me and for always supporting my crazy ideas. I love you.

Dad—I learned many of the lessons in this book by simply watching the way you live your life. I am so grateful.

Lion—You make me want to be a better man. I'm about to go work out so that I can still take you down when I'm seventy.

Connor Crumpton and Grant Skeldon—Thanks for being some of my best friends and letting me flesh out many of these ideas with you. You are true brothers.

Jonathan Pokluda—For writing the foreword. Very few people have been as openhanded and encouraging to me on my journey. Thank you for letting me learn from you!

Thomas Dean—You're the best agent on the planet. Thank you for being such a kind, wise, and encouraging friend. This book would literally not be possible without you!

Way Church—You're the most amazing community on the planet, and it's such an honor to be your pastor. Thank you for your grace, love, and support for me and my family.

Andy McGuire—You're a new friend and one I hope will be forever. Thank you for taking a chance on a young author like me and for believing in me!

acknowledgments

The Bethany House team—What a joy it has been to work with such an amazing group of people on two books now. The work you all do is a reflection of the people you are. Thank you for making this experience such a great one and for bringing this dream to life.

about the author

_Noah Herrin is a pastor, communicator, and author based in Nashville, Tennessee. He serves as the lead pastor of Way Church in the heart of Nashville and has become a trusted voice in the Gen Z and Millennial online space and at churches, conferences, universities, and businesses around the world, helping to train and mentor the next generation of leaders. Founder of The Gathering Conference, he's the author of *Viral Jesus*, *Holy Habits*, and now *Welcome to Manhood*. Noah and his wife, Maddy, have three children: Lion, Mila, and Navy. In his free time, he enjoys spending time with his family and playing golf.

Connect with Noah:

- 🌐 NoahHerrin.org
- ⓕ facebook.com/Noah.Herrin
- ⓘ @noahherrin
- ⓧ @NoahHerrin